Embroidery and Fabric Collage

CHANGING SEASONS, by Eirian Short

Embroidery and Fabric Collage

EIRIAN SHORT

CHARLES SCRIBNER'S SONS
NEW YORK

SBN 684–12923–x

Made and printed in Great Britain by
William Clowes & Sons, Limited, London, Beccles and Colchester
Library of Congress Catalog Card Number 77–39840
A–2.72 (I)

Preface

THROUGHOUT the book the term embroidery is used in its widest sense, as the embellishment of a surface of fabric with some form of decoration carried out with the needle and thread. Thus, the meaning is not confined to traditional methods of embroidery, with their conventions born of long usage: neither does it exclude simple forms of sewing such as patchwork and appliqué. No one method is considered superior to another: no special virtue attached to, say, hand embroidery as opposed to machine embroidery, or gold work as opposed to quilting. The only criterion is that the method chosen should be the most suitable in that particular set of circumstances, and that the final result be satisfactory.

Although the true meaning of collage is that of pasting or gluing, in the case of *fabric collage* it has taken on a looser meaning. The term fabric collage is generally understood to mean the application of pieces of fabric to a background, whether by sticking or sewing, and with little or no surface embroidery. It is usually used in pictures, panels and hangings, being unsuitable for practical purposes.

It will be found that, throughout the book, certain theories are expounded and rules laid down, but none should be taken as absolutely categorical. In the hands of an experienced designer or truly creative artist, any so called rule can be broken provided the end justifies it. It is always the result which is the final criterion. However, rules do serve to guide the novice until, through experience, the possibilities and limitations of the medium are thoroughly understood.

Embroidery can be appreciated on many different levels, and in our society there is a considerable gulf between applied decoration on everyday objects and embroidery used as a medium of artistic expression. In primitive societies this gulf does not exist. The primitive expresses his religious beliefs, his fears and superstitions in the decoration of his everyday utensils, clothes and ornaments. By means of symbols he can embroider a pattern which is both decorative and expressive. In our more sophisticated society the two have become separated, and it is unusual to find work of serious artistic or religious intent on articles of everyday use. Indeed we should feel uncomfortable if this were so. Embroidery as a means of expression, as "fine art," is, therefore, dealt with separately in Chapter Four, and includes pictures, panels, hangings and ecclesiastical embroidery.

Acknowledgements

I should like to thank all those who have helped me compile this book. Practising artists and students have generously lent their work or photographs of their work. Museums and other institutions have given me permission to reproduce work from their collections. My sincere thanks go to the following:

The Victoria and Albert Museum for permission to reproduce Plates 2, 16, 31 lower and Figures 39 and 40; The Vatican Museum for Plate 1; The American Museum in Britain for Plate 17; William Briggs & Co Ltd for Plate 23 upper; Copthall Grammar School, London, for Plate 26; The Crafts Council of Great Britain for Plates 34 and 35; The Embroiderers' Guild for Plates 14 upper, 18, 20 lower and 21; Leicestershire Education Committee for Plate 25 upper; Mr P. F. Millard for work by students at Goldsmiths College, School of Art, Plates 5 upper and lower right and 32; The Musée Matisse, Vence, and S.P.A.D.E.M. of Paris for Plate 36; The Penrose Collection and S.P.A.D.E.M. of Paris for Plate 31 upper; Miss M. E. Puddephat, M.Ed., for work by students at the Rachel McMillan Training College, Plates 13, 14 lower and 19; Mr H. H. Shelton, A.R.C.A., A.R.E., F.S.A., A.S.I.A., N.R.D., for work by students at Hornsey College of Art, Plates 8 and 9.

My thanks also to the following individuals for the loan of work or photographs:

Anne Butler, Ioné Dorrington, Tecla Finck, Rosalynd Floyd, Constance Howard, Margaret Kaye, Sue Kemp, George Pace, Pat Phillpott, Anne Preston, Selina Rand, Christine Risley and Sally Scott.

Lastly I should like to thank John Minshall who helped me so much with the photography.

Contents

Plates

Plates—CONTINUED

Plates—CONTINUED

Plates—CONTINUED

Chapter One

Design

ENGLISH embroidery has at times been the medium for work of the highest creative order; at other times it has degenerated into a mere pastime. During the Golden Age, in the thirteenth and fourteenth centuries, England produced ecclesiastical and secular embroideries of such a high standard that they were sought after by churches and noble families throughout Europe. Well designed and beautifully executed, "Opus Anglicanum" had that overall concept which distinguishes a work of art from one of mere expertise. Much can be learned about the nature of good embroidery by comparing a piece of work from this period with one from the mid-Victorian era, a time when embroidery design was generally poor.

The two works chosen for comparison are a detail of the Vatican Cope and a Berlin Woolwork picture (Plates 1 & 2). The two pieces are religious in subject; both incorporate the human figure; both are technically well executed; but here the resemblance ends. Whereas one is uplifting to look at the other leaves one emotionally cold. In the Opus Anglicanum the stitches are used with a purpose, emphasizing the forms, while in the Victorian picture they are just a repetitive way of "filling in" the ready-made design. In the medieval work the figures are conceived as a motif, designed to fill the space which it occupies, and make an interesting, expressive pattern within that shape. The Berlin Woolwork, on the other hand, treats the figures in an unselective, naturalistic way, and, by using shading and perspective, attempts a realistic portrayal out of place in embroidery. There is also a cheap attempt at realism in the working of the ermine robe in a pile stitch, simulating real fur. The Vatican Cope was

1. Opus Anglicanum. Crucifixion. Detail from the Vatican Cope (1280 A.D.–1300 A.D.).
(*By courtesy of the Vatican Museum*)

obviously conceived from the beginning as an embroidery, whereas the Berlin Woolwork picture is merely a copy of a painting in the medium of embroidery.

From the comparison of these two works certain deductions may be made which will act as a guide to designing for embroidery in general.

1. Stitches must be used as a means of expression and not as an end in themselves. When stitches are used for their own sake, just for the pleasure of working them, or as a way of filling in a ready-made design, then embroidery ceases to be a creative medium.

2. The work should be conceived from the beginning as an embroidery and not copied blindly from another medium. Every art form has its own characteristics and it is these that

2. BERLIN WOOL-WORK: "JOSEPH PRESENTING HIS FATHER TO PHARAOH." (1885)
(*By courtesy of the Victoria and Albert Museum*)

give it its particular quality and flavour. Embroidery in this country has been at its worst when it has tried to imitate painting instead of developing its own qualities. (Mary Linwood's copies of oil paintings in the eighteenth century are an example of this.) Using another medium as a source of ideas is another matter altogether. The design is then *based* on the other medium but worked out in terms of embroidery. It is a translation, not an imitation.

3. Design for embroidery should be thought of as flat pattern and not as naturalistic representation. Shading, to give a feeling of roundness, and vanishing-point perspective are out of place. Embroidery is, essentially, the *embellishment of a surface* of cloth and anything which tends to destroy the integrity of that surface is false to the medium. This

3. EXPERIMENTAL PANEL USING FELT IN HIGH RELIEF. As one fabric is used throughout, there are no contrasts of colour or texture, and the design relies for interest on the tonal pattern made by the shadows

point is of great importance and should be thoroughly understood. It can be further elucidated, perhaps, by analogy with painting. In one kind of painting the picture surface is a window through which one looks into a view of the subject, whether it be landscape, still life or portrait. The other approach is to treat the flat surface of the canvas or board as the important factor and keep all the components of the pictorial composition on that plane. This is the most usual approach in painting today and that most suited to embroidery. From this it must not be supposed that the surface of the fabric must be kept flat *physically*, i.e. that stitches and material must not be built up. It is a *pictorial* three-dimensional quality which is to be avoided, not an actual one.

4. If good embroidery were just a matter of executing stitches well, then the Berlin Woolwork would rank with the Opus Anglicanum. As it so patently does not it must be concluded that the difference lies in the overall conception of the work.

A certain amount of technical ability is obviously necessary in order to be able to express an idea in terms of embroidery, but it is the *idea itself* which is the most important factor.

Learning to design for any art form or craft is analogous to learning a new language. Before one can express one-self fluently in that language the vocabulary and grammar must be learnt. The "vocabulary" in the case of embroidery consists of the hundreds of stitches and many different techniques at the embroiderer's disposal. These have been adequately covered in many books on embroidery and it is not intended to repeat them here. A list of useful reference books is given on page 123. What is aimed at is a "grammar;" an analysis of the components of good design, their construction and their integration into a work of art.

It is difficult to learn to speak a language solely from books. Constant practice in conversation is needed in order to become fluent. For the design student too, theoretical knowledge is not enough. Theories must be tried out and tested before they can successfully be put into practice.

The first essential in designing for any medium is a thorough knowledge of the qualities inherent in the materials used. As a sculptor learns to appreciate the characteristics of clay, wood, stone and metal, the embroiderer must realize, through experience, both the great possibilities and the limitations of fabric and thread. The following experiment should be carried out: a scrap of coloured fabric should be placed on to a sheet of paper and studied to ascertain its most important properties. These are some of the things which become obvious—

1. The piece of fabric has *shape*, i.e. it may be round or square or irregular.

2. It has *colour* (hue), for example it may be green or red or blue.

3. It also has *tonal value*, it is lighter or darker than the paper on which it is lying.

4. It has *texture*, its surface is rough or smooth, shiny or dull, closely or openly woven.

Fig. 1. *Upper:* Symmetry in Nature (snow crystal)

Lower: Symmetrical Design Geometrically Constructed

Fig. 2 (*right*). The "See-Saw" Principle of Balance. The greater weight is placed nearer the centre

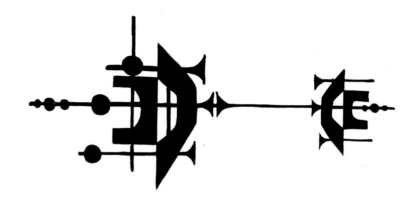

Fig. 3 (*below*). Motifs
A motif is rarely seen in isolation. As soon as it is placed within another shape (*centre*) or with other motifs (*bottom*) a new set of shapes is created by the spaces

Shape

Generally speaking we are more aware of shape than we are of colour, tone or texture. A young child, given a set of bricks of different shapes and colours and told to pair them, will put together a red square and a blue square rather than two reds of different shapes. In other words, the *shape* of the brick is more important to him than the *colour*. Indeed, primitive man depended very largely for his survival on his ability to pick out the shapes of animals against the landscape; the silhouette of a friend in the street is recognizable long before he is near enough for the colour of his hair and eyes to be seen. Shape, therefore, is of primary importance. Attractive colour, however beguiling to the senses, is wasted unless the structure of the design is sound.

Shapes have weight and need to be balanced to make a pleasant, unified design. The most obvious form of balanced design is the symmetrical one, where both halves of the design exactly correspond and, therefore, must balance. Many symmetrical forms are found in nature, e.g. crystalline structures and snowflake patterns (Fig. 1). Both were used extensively as sources of embroidery design in the Swedish-influenced period after the Second World War. Symmetrical designs give a stiff, rather formal appearance, and symmetrical motifs can be given a more lively quality by being grouped asymmetrically. There are times, of course, when a simple, formal effect is called for, and then symmetrical motifs, and repeat patterns, come into their own.

Asymmetric designs offer endless permutations of arrangements of shapes: balancing one large shape with several small ones, contrasting a solid shape with a linear one, etc. One

Fig. 4. Complete Alternation Between Figure and Ground
The design can be read as two white faces in profile on a black ground, or as a black urn on a white ground. This is known as a "negative-positive" design

principle of balance can be understood by watching children on a seesaw. If the children are of equal weight they sit at equal distances from the central point of balance. If one child is heavier then he must sit nearer the centre in order not to outbalance the lighter child. The same principle holds good when composing an arrangement of shapes. A heavy shape near the centre of the design will be balanced by a much less heavy shape near the outer edge. The design in Fig. 2 is a simplified example, but the same feeling of right placing should prevail in the most complicated design. A well balanced design should give a feeling of inevitability, and "rightness", a feeling that this is the only possible arrangement for this particular set of shapes.

As soon as one or more shapes are set down in a given area they create other shapes (Fig. 3). These secondary shapes are also important and should never be thought of as merely background, but as part of the whole pattern which is being created. There is a popular "trick" diagram (Fig. 4) which can be read in two ways: (a) as two faces in profile, facing one another on a black background or (b) as a black urn on a white background. This complete alternation between figure and ground is admittedly an exaggerated instance, but it does bring home the point. Any space created by putting down a shape in a given area must be considered as an integral part of the pattern being made. This point cannot be emphasized too strongly. It is easy when drawing, say, a spray of leaves, to think only of the shapes of the leaves, and not to consider the spaces in between them. But we have seen that those spaces are just as

Fig. 5. Hungarian Peasant Embroidery
This can be read as light squares on a dark background or as dark star shapes on light ground

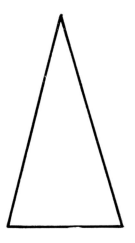

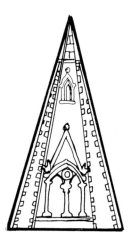

Fig. 6. Symbolic Association of a Triangle with Hands Uplifted in Prayer and with a Church Spire

important and must be considered just as carefully as the leaves themselves or the finished design will not work successfully as a surface pattern.

The shapes within a design should bear some relationship to one another if the design is to have unity. A collection of unrelated shapes cannot be called a design, the very word implies order. Related shapes need not become boring, there can be variations and contrasts while still keeping a "family resemblance" (Fig. 22).

As well as their visual aspect, shapes have symbolic significance. This may be intrinsic in the shape. A circle, for instance, having no beginning and no end gives a feeling of completeness. The symbolism may be by association. A triangle can give a feeling of striving upward, of communication with God, partly because of its intrinsic shape, but also because of its association with hands in prayer, or a church spire (Fig. 6). Of course, the church spire may have been made that way in the first place to propagate that very feeling. The direction which a shape takes is very important. A square placed straight creates a static feeling, a tranquil mood. Tipped on its side there is immediately a feeling of restlessness, movement. In other words, the use of the horizontal and vertical gives stability to a design, the use of diagonals gives dynamism, unrest (Fig. 7).

All these factors must be considered when planning a design. It is not enough to think "I will draw a spray of leaves," or "I will make a design composed entirely of triangles," without realizing what effect they will have when translated into a two-dimensional design.

A decorative motif or set of motifs must always be considered in relation to the shape which contains them. Thus,

Fig. 7. Square on the Horizontal and Vertical Gives a Feeling of Calm; Tipped, it Suggests Restlessness, Energy

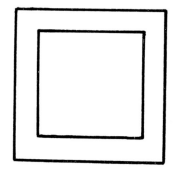

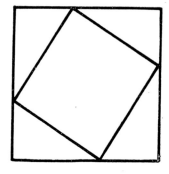

Fig. 8. Relating a Motif to its
Background
Top: Motif is too small, there is no
connection with the outer edge.
Centre: Motif is right size but
appears to be moving out of the
bottom right-hand corner.
Bottom: Satisfactory size and placing

however well the units in a design balance each other, the effect will be ruined unless the relationship to the outside shape is also good. In Fig. 8 (top) the motif, although satisfactory in itself, is too small in relation to the outside edge, so that the spaces around the motif are not felt to be part of the design. As we have seen in Fig. 3 these shapes are very important. In Fig. 8 (centre) the scale is more satisfactory, but the motif is placed too near the bottom right-hand corner and there is a feeling of the motif being pulled out of that corner. In Fig. 8 (bottom) the size and positioning are satisfactory and there is a feeling of pattern over the whole surface of the square.

Colour and Tone

It is important to distinguish between colour and tone. The colour of a piece of fabric or thread is its hue, i.e. whether it is brown or blue or yellow. Its tone (brilliance), on the other hand, is its comparative lightness or darkness. One colour, for instance crimson, can be used in an infinite number of tones, from its full strength down to a pale pink, but it is still basically the same colour. On the other hand several colours, for example a blue, a green and a red, could be exactly the same in tone, that is to say, one would be no lighter and no darker than the others. It is easy to assess the relative tone values of strong contrasts, such as black and white, but when the tones are close it is advisable to look through almost closed eyes, until the colour practically disappears, and the tonal relationship becomes more obvious.

Using paint, coloured paper, or scraps of fabric the following experiment may be carried out. If on a dark purple background is placed a small square of (*a*) white, and (*b*) navy blue, two things should become obvious. That (1) whereas it is easy to see which is the darker in the case of purple and white, the task is much more difficult in the case of purple and navy blue; and (2) the white square shows up as a distinct *shape*, but one has to look more closely to see the shape of the navy blue square.

There is a practical application to this. If the finished piece of embroidery is to be seen from a distance, as for instance a wall hanging, then a design using strong contrasts of tone will have greater impact. If, on the other hand, the embroidery is not intended to be too obvious, as on a dress, then close tones will give a more subtle effect.

MAKING A COLOUR WHEEL

Making a colour wheel serves two purposes. Much will be learned about the properties of colours while making it, and when complete, it will be a useful source of reference. The simplest form of colour wheel is one containing the three primary colours (Fig. 9A). These are red, blue and yellow. It is not enough, however, to use any red, any blue and any yellow. The red should be a pure red, that is to say it should not be a red which contains blue (i.e. crimson), or a red which contains yellow (i.e. vermilion). The blue should not contain yellow (i.e. turquoise) or red (i.e. ultramarine) and the yellow should not contain red (i.e. yellow ochre) or blue (i.e. lemon). This task will not be easy and some time will probably be spent before the pure colours are achieved, but much will be learnt about handling colour in the process. These three pure colours are the three *primary colours* from which all other colours are made. By mixing any pair of primary colours a new colour is produced, known as a *secondary colour* and this is "complementary" to the remaining primary in the colour wheel. Thus, red and blue mixed give violet, which is complementary to yellow; yellow and blue give green, which is complementary to red; and red and yellow give orange, which is complementary to blue. Pairs of complementaries are colours which are as different from one another as is possible and, therefore, give a lively vibrating effect. (Think of red berries against green leaves; an orange dinghy against a blue sea.) Placed side by side they exact the maximum vividness from each other, mixed together, in pigment, they give a neutral grey.

A second colour wheel can now be constructed with six divisions (Fig. 9B), putting in violet, which is a mixture of the two between red and blue, and so on. It will be noted that the pairs of complementaries come directly opposite one another in the wheel.

Between any two colours there could obviously be an infinite number of gradations from one to the other, but for practical purposes a wheel with twelve sections, inserting one "half-way" colour between each primary and secondary colour will be found adequate. Thus between blue and green there will be a bluey-green (turquoise), etc. Remembering that complementary colours lie opposite one another it will

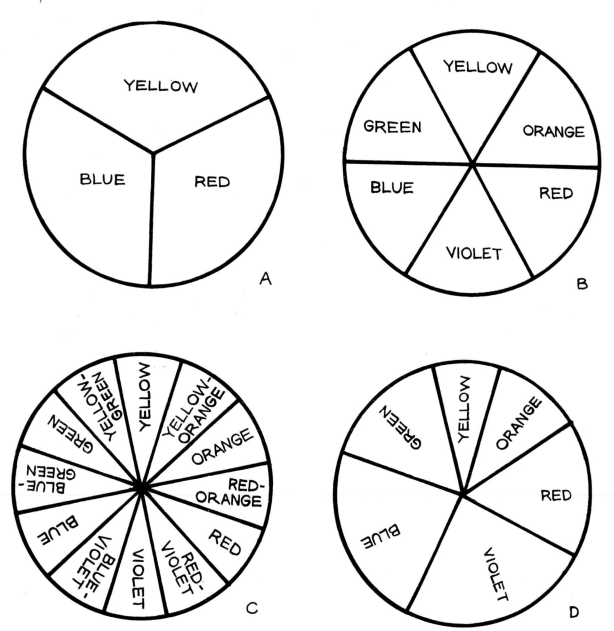

Fig. 9. Colour Wheels: (A) Primary Colours, (B) Secondary Colours (complementaries), (C) Twelve-section Colour Wheel, (D) Balanced Proportions of Colours

now become apparent that the true complementary of a blue red is a yellow green, and that of a yellow red is a blue green etc. (Fig. 9C).

A mixture of all three primary colours results in *tertiary colours*. These are the subtle colours such as khaki, various browns, etc., and are excellent foils for the clear, bright primary and secondary colours. Experiments in mixing the three primaries in different proportions will result in a wide variety of subtle colours. A predominance of yellow in the mixture will give a range of khakis, a predominance of red will give browns, a predominance of blue gives exciting dark blue-greens. A mixture of the three primaries in certain proportions is the equivalent of a mixture of two complementaries and will, therefore, give a neutral grey. Grey can also be mixed from black and white, the only other neutrals. In the colour wheel the hues are all used at their full strength or saturation, i.e. they are not diluted in any way by black or white. The addition of white to a colour, in varying amounts, produces a range of "tints," paler versions of the original colour; the addition of black, "shades," darker tones of the colour. In a design, the effect of too many colours of full strength can be overpowering, and it is often more satisfactory to combine some areas of diluted colour, either tints or shades, with strong colours.

On closer study of the colour wheel further facts should become apparent. Some colours give a feeling of warmth, some of coldness. Colours containing red look warm, those containing blue look cold. But red itself if it contains a lot of blue can look comparatively cool (crimson), and a blue that contains red can look warm (ultramarine). These facts are important when planning colour schemes for interior decoration. For instance a cold room can be given an appearance of warmth by using reds, oranges, and warm yellows, while a too sunny room can appear cool if blues and greens are used.

Another look at the colour wheel will show that yellow is the colour lightest in tone, and violet is the darkest. When colours are used undiluted this is the natural order of things. From yellow to violet on either side of the wheel there is a gradual darkening. If any two colours are taken and this natural tonal relationship reversed then a discord results. For instance, blue is normally darker than green, so if a pale blue is put against a dark green the result will give a scintillating discord. A discordant colour scheme which has been very popular in the early 'sixties is that of orange and pink. Normally red is darker than orange, but when enough white is added to turn it into a pink, lighter than the orange, a discord results. Experiments can be made with various other combinations of colour discords.

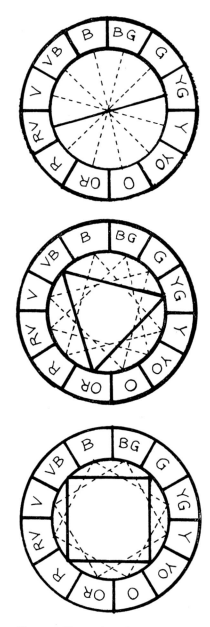

Fig. 10. Harmonious Colour Schemes. *Top:* Dyads, *Centre:* Triads, *Bottom:* Tetrads

COLOUR HARMONY

Much has been written about colour harmony. Harmonious colour schemes were at one time defined as those lying adjacent on the colour wheel; for instance, red violet and blue, or red, orange and yellow. These certainly do give harmony of a kind, but in a very limited way, and far more exciting combinations can be tried out. Colour is an intensely personal element in design and what will appear as a harmonious scheme to one person may elicit no response in another. There are, however, certain rules of thumb for constructing harmonious combinations of colours, but these can be endlessly varied by altering the relative tones of the colours concerned.

1. *Dyads.* These are any two colours diametrically opposite to one another in the colour wheel. In other words, the complementaries. We have seen that complementary pairs of colours are lively and vibrant. They are also satisfying to the eye in that they contain all three primary colours. A colour scheme containing only two primaries, say yellow and green, "demands" a colour containing red in order to complete the balance of colour in the viewer's eye.

2. *Triads.* Any three colours in the circle whose position forms an equilateral triangle give a harmonious colour scheme. The most obvious is yellow, red and blue, the three primaries: instead can be tried violet, orange and green; yellow green, red orange and blue violet, etc.

3. *Tetrads.* These are colours lying at the four corners of a square within the colour circle, and within a twelve-hue colour circle there are only three possible combinations (Fig. 10).

It must be stressed again that in any of the above colour schemes the results will be far more interesting and satisfying if the colours are used at varying strengths, i.e. with either white or black added. It will be seen from the colour wheel that when the colours are present in equal quantities as they are on the wheel, that yellow, because of its brilliance, predominates, while violet being dark in tone is the least conspicuous. Orange stands out more than blue, but red and green are about equal. Thus, it becomes obvious that if yellow is used in a design it must be used in small quantities if it is not to dominate the colour scheme completely. As a *rough* guide it may be said that colours should be used in the following proportions to ensure a balanced colour scheme. Taking pairs of complementaries, violet to yellow should be in a ratio of three to one, blue to orange in the ratio of two to one, and red and green equal. A diagram of a balanced colour wheel, using these proportions as a guide, is shown in Fig. 9D.

Effects of depth can be created with colour. If the three primary colours are placed on a black background the yellow will appear to float in the foreground, the red will come forward, but not as much as the yellow, while the blue appears to cling to the background. This is due to the relative brilliance, or tone value of the three colours. If the three primaries are placed on a white background the reverse will happen—the darker colour (blue) will come forward, the yellow will appear furthest from the eye. If several colours of similar brilliance are placed together, the warm colours appear to advance and the cold to recede. The qualities of any colour are only valid in relation to other colours lying near. The same violet colour can look blue when placed next to red and red when placed next to blue. Tonal relationships too are relative; the same area of mid-toned hue can look dark against a white background, but light against a dark background. This means that when planning a design the tonal relationship and colour scheme of the whole must be kept in mind all the time.

The effect which colours have on the onlooker goes far beyond liking or disliking a particular combination. Most colours have symbolic associations—red suggests blood, blue the sky or sea, green growing things, etc. Abstract concepts, too, may be conjured up, purity by white, pomp by purple, death by black. The different seasons of the year are associated in our minds with different colours, and colours with no direct symbolic significance can, by their intrinsic character, create a mood or climate.

The designer should be prepared to spend some time in carrying out colour exercises. It is only by constant experiment that fresh and exciting colour schemes will be evolved. The most dynamic colour combination if used too often loses

4. SELF-COLOUR EMBROIDERY IN WHICH TEXTURE PLAYS AN IMPORTANT PART. *Top left:* Cut work; *Centre left:* English quilting; *Bottom left:* Pulled work (drawn fabric); *Bottom right:* Net darning

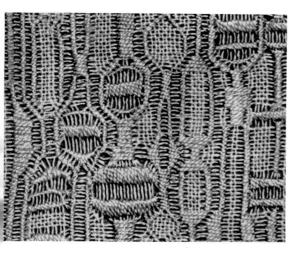

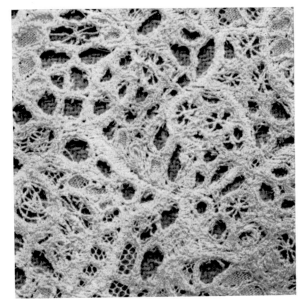

5. TEXTURES.
Left: Textures Produced by Hand. *Above:* Honeycombing; *Below:* Needleweaving
Right: Interesting Textures Produced on the Domestic Sewing Machine, by Josephine Canty, student at Goldsmiths' College School of Art. *Above:* Darning on Lace; *Below:* Whip stitch.

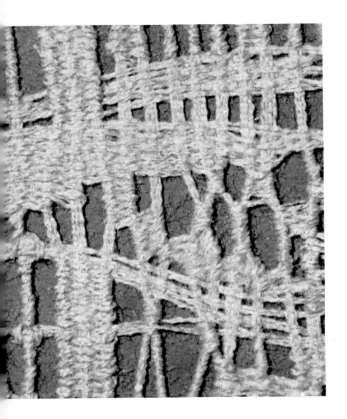

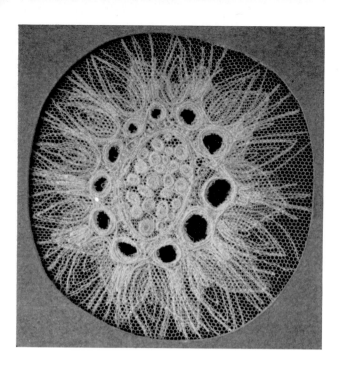
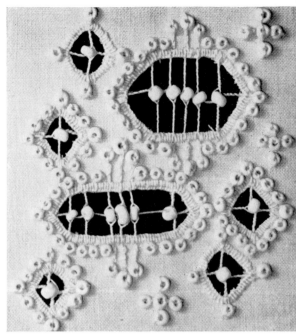

6. *Top left:* Motif on Net with Machine Darning and Cut Work; *Top right:* Combination of Cut Work and Beading; *Bottom left:* Indian "Shisha" or Mirror Embroidery; *Bottom right:* Canvas Sampler including Surrey Stitch which forms a Pile.

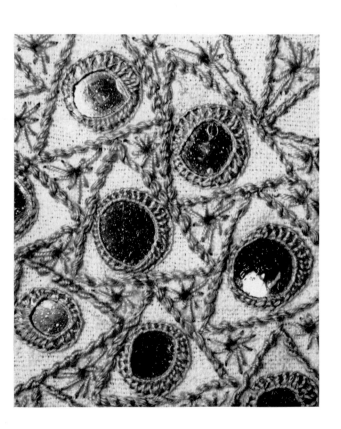

its impact. Colours which shocked a few years ago are now accepted, and commonly found on furnishing and dress fabric. It is not always necessary to work out colour schemes on paper—a bundle of threads or fabrics accidentally thrown together may suggest an exciting scheme; so may some outdoor object lighted on by chance. A pool of oil in the road, a piece of rusted up metal, a weathered poster on a hoarding, any of these could be noted in a sketch-book and kept for future reference. Nature, too, furnishes countless ideas: in markings on an animal, in the shadow under a tree, on a pebble or in rock strata, at the bottom of a pool, subtle combinations of colours and tones are to be found. Groups of people make interesting splashes of colour. Notice children playing in a playground, footballers on the heath, bathers coming out of the sea. Colour is everywhere, it is up to the individual to learn to see it.

Texture

Texture is essentially a quality ascertained by touch, but it can also be visually perceived. The word texture comes from the same root as textile, and in the strictest sense means the surface quality of a piece of cloth. The term is now more loosely applied to mean the surface quality of any substance, e.g. wood, stone, fur, etc. Texture is a factor which plays a very important part in modern architecture and interior decoration. A look round a well-designed room of the present day may show a shaggy rug on a polished wood floor, rough tweed cushions on a leather settee, or open net against walls of glass. This interest in texture is also evident in painting and sculpture of the present time. Think of tachiste paintings with the paint dribbled on, paintings built up into reliefs with strips of wood and plaster, stone carving polished to a glass-like smoothness, metal constructions with intricate surfaces of nuts and bolts.

Fabrics and threads are rich in contrasting textures, and different combinations should be tried out and critically assessed. It will be found that whereas felt against felt looks lifeless, felt against nubbly tweed relieves the "busy" texture of the tweed and enhances it. In the same way a matt surface such as crêpe or wool can be livened up by the

Summer Rain, by Christine Risley

use of small areas of a shiny material such as satin. It would appear that any texture, however interesting in itself, is enhanced by contrast. Of course, contrasting textures are not only found in ready-made materials, but can be produced by different methods of embroidery. Many traditional methods of embroidery rely for their interest on changing the original surface texture of the fabric.

1. *Cut work, Broderie Anglaise and Hedebo embroidery*. These all entail cutting away part of the ground fabric. Significantly, they are all worked on closely-woven fabric, so that the open spaces form a direct contrast with the background. Further texture is added by surface stitchery and occasionally, padded edgings to the holes.

2. *Quilting*. In all forms of quilting, English, Italian and Trapunto, the otherwise flat surface of the material is transformed by means of padding into an undulating surface.

3. *Pulled work or drawn fabric*. Here the even warp and weft of the fabric are pulled and distorted to form both holes in the fabric and raised patterns on the surface. The embroidery completely alters the original plain-woven texture of the material.

4. *Casalguidi embroidery*. This is an old Italian embroidery which superimposes highly-raised stitches on a drawn-fabric background, thus providing two changes in texture.

5. *Mountmellick embroidery*. This embroidery relies on padded stitches, knots, etc., giving a raised surface to the embroidery.

6. *Net darning, fillet darning*. These methods of embroidery reverse the procedure of cut work. Here the original fabric is open in texture and the embroidery consists of closing up this open texture in parts by means of various filling stitches. (Plate 4.)

It is significant that nearly all the above embroideries are usually worked in white or self colour. In these circumstances the texture becomes the all important factor, for there

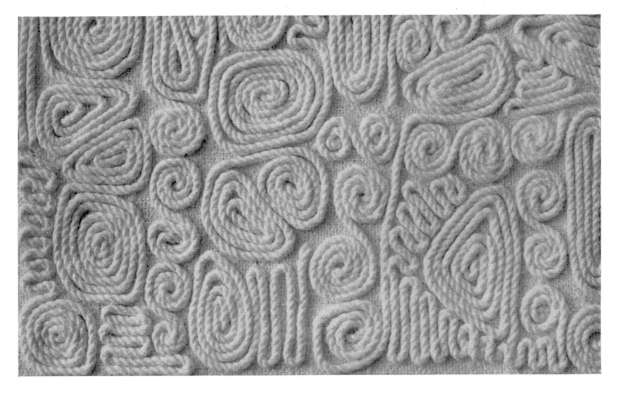

7. *Top:* ALLOVER PATTERN IN PIPING CORD ON WHITE LINEN. This type of pattern, with no regular repeat, could be adapted for many uses on dress, dress accessories or household articles

Bottom: TRAPUNTO. Worked on the domestic sewing machine through two thicknesses of fabric and afterwards padded by slitting the backing and inserting cotton wool

is no colour to excite the eye, no strongly contrasting tones to make patterns on the background. For interest the embroidery relies on the shadows cast by the stitches in high relief and padding, or the dark patterns of holes in the fabric.

Conversely, most of the embroidery mentioned above is spoilt if worked in multi-colours. This applies particularly to net darning and all the different kinds of cut work, which completely lose their lacy quality and become muddled and confusing. Glaring examples of this can be found in so many of the cut-work designs on sale to the public.

It makes an interesting exercise to select six fabrics and completely transform the surface texture of each by some kind of embroidery, for instance smooth satin stitches on a rough fabric, cut work on finely woven lawn, or knotted stitches on a smooth fabric.

The materials at the disposal of the embroiderer today, in the way of fabrics of all kinds, threads, raffia, beads, braids, and ribbons are so rich and varied that there is no excuse for producing work which is dull and monotonous in texture.

Flat Pattern

In the past a striving after naturalism has given rise to the worst kind of embroidery. Attempting to give a feeling of three dimensions by the use of shading and perspective is contrary to the true nature of embroidery design. How much more suitable is the "flat pattern" used by the designers of Opus Anglicanum and Elizabethan embroideries. What then is meant by flat pattern? How is flat pattern to be achieved when depicting things which in real life are three dimensional—"in the round?" This can be explained by taking a simple example, the cube. It is a Western convention, especially since the Renaissance to draw in vanishing-

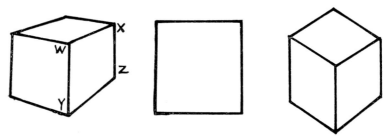

Fig. 11. Cube Drawn *left*, in Vanishing-point Perspective, *centre*, Looking Flat on to one Side, *right*, by Isometric Projection

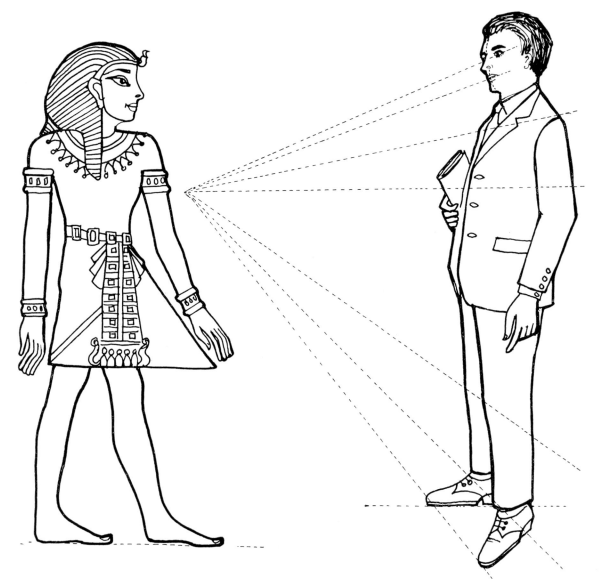

Fig. 12. Figure Drawn *left*, in the Egyptian Manner, *right*, in the Western Manner, Using Vanishing-point Perspective

point perspective. Perspective is the art of drawing solid objects on to a two-dimensional plane (canvas, sheet of paper) so as to produce the appearance of the actual object as viewed from one point. Although this gives an appearance of reality it will be seen from the cube in Fig. 11 (*left*) that the lines WX and XZ are shorter than WY and YZ. Now all the sides of a cube are, in reality, equal, so the truth is being distorted in order to give what is felt to be a true representation.

Fig. 13. Three Treatments of Hands Holding a Brush or Pen. *Top*, "Naturalistic" Drawing, *centre*, by a Ninth Century Monk, and *bottom*, as if by Picasso

Children, Eastern civilizations, and primitive peoples have other solutions to the problem. They either take the simplest view, looking directly on to one side of the cube, leaving the imagination, supplemented by past knowledge, to fill in the rest, or they use an "isometric projection" which explains the cube without distortion (Figs. 11 (*centre* and *right*)).

The problem of foreshortening, seen in the cube, i.e. the apparent shortening of receding lines, also crops up in the drawing of natural forms and the human figure. If the human figure is seen from the side, the shoulders recede and therefore appear foreshortened. If the figure is seen from the front the feet present a similar problem, and so on. Consequently drawing a figure in the Western manner, from one viewpoint, is bound to present problems of foreshortening and perspective. In the "Egyptian" way of drawing these problems are overcome by drawing *each part* of the figure from the most advantageous view. The head is drawn from the side, eliminating difficulties with the nose, but the eye in that head is seen from the front, explaining the whole eye, and, incidentally, making a more decorative shape. The shoulders are seen from the front, but at the waist the torso is turned so that the legs and feet may be drawn from the side. Despite all this, the figure has a unity and comes over perfectly convincingly (Fig. 12). In this type of drawing the artist is portraying what he knows to exist, rather than what he actually sees. It must not be thought that the Egyptians drew in this way because they did not have the technical ability to draw in the "Western manner." They may have drawn without perspective in the beginning because of a lack of knowledge, but continued to do so for thousands of years, partly because it became a convention, rigidly adhered to, but also probably because of the inherent strength and decorative qualities of this kind of drawing. All drawing is a matter of making symbols, and the front view of an eye is the most powerful symbol of an eye, the side view of a foot, the most characteristic of the foot, etc.

Although we speak glibly of "naturalistic" drawing, the most naturalistic is still only a series of light or dark marks on paper which are "read" by the onlooker as the subject portrayed. Really primitive people who have never seen a photograph, when shown a bunch of bananas and the photograph of a bunch of bananas cannot see any connection

Fig. 14. The Head Depicted by (A) and (C) Primitive Man, (B) Picasso, (D) a Mediaeval Embroiderer, (E) a Ninth Century Monk, and (F) a Boy of Five

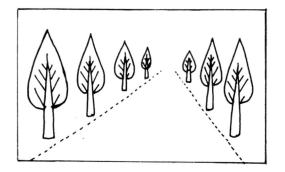  

Fig. 15.   Distance Portrayed by *left*, Vanishing-point Perspective, *centre*, Variation in Size, *right*, Overlapping

between the two. To them bananas are solid objects, a photograph is a flat piece of card with marks on it. In other words, they have not learnt to "read" a photograph. We, on the other hand, have learned from early childhood to interpret photographs and, similarly, drawings in the western manner. The particular type of drawing which we regard as a naturalistic representation is one which uses vanishing-point perspective, shading to suggest roundness, cast shadows, etc., or a line drawing in which the roundness of the form is suggested by the contours. It must be realized that this is just our particular convention; that the child's way of depicting a head (Fig. 14F) or the stylized pattern of the primitive (Figs. 14A and C) or Picasso's combination of front face and profile in the same drawing (Fig. 14B) are all equally valid as symbols for heads. The primitive would regard his drawings as realistic and find the western style more difficult to interpret.

In embroidery it is necessary to find a way of depicting a head (or figure, or flower) so that it is a meaningful symbol, at the same time making a flat decorative pattern.

Another problem is how to depict spacial relationship (the relative distances of objects from the eye) without destroying the flatness of the picture plane. The two simplest methods are by gradation in size (Fig. 15 (*centre*)) and overlapping (Fig. 15 (*right*)).

Sometimes shading and perspective are deliberately made use of as in the traditional patchwork design known as "box pattern" (Fig. 16 (*left*)). They are, however, used in such a way as to make a decorative pattern, and not to give a feeling of reality as in the drawing of the cotton reel in Fig. 16 (*right*).

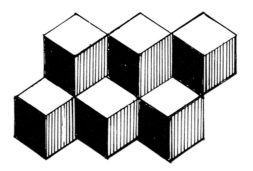

Fig. 16. Shading and Perspective
Left, Used deliberately in a flat and decorative way (the popular box pattern used in patchwork); and *right*, used to give a naturalistic three-dimensional quality. The former is more suitable to embroidery

Sources of Design

Almost any subject can be used as a successful basis for an embroidery design, provided it is not treated realistically or sentimentally. Human figures, animals, plants, fish, birds, fruit, vegetables, gemstones, rocks, trees, the solar system, water, fire—these are some of the aspects of nature which could be the starting point for designs. Man-made objects, too—buildings, wrought-iron, wood carvings etc., can be the inspiration for design. It is interesting to take one subject and see how many different aspects of it can be used as a basis for design. A tree, for instance, would yield patterns from the silhouette, both in leaf and bare; from the individual leaves; from a cross section of the trunk; from the roots and bark. Microscopic enlargements of the cellular structure, or even magnification of the wood under a strong magnifying glass would provide further ideas. The same principle can, of course, be applied to any subject matter. Animals, fish, reptiles, etc., are particularly rich sources of design with their markings, feathers, manes and other decorative features. When the outside appearances of objects have been fully exploited, there are other aspects which will provide ideas for designs. Skeletons of fish, birds and small animals are extremely delicate and beautiful. The skull of a rabbit or cat; the skeleton of a fish or bird can often be picked up on the seashore and can make an excellent subject for detailed studies, from which designs can later be evolved. For designers living in London, the Fossil Rooms at the Natural History Museum offer countless ideas. Fruit and vegetables cut through at different angles give a variety of patterns. The pattern of a slice of tomato, for instance, cut across is completely different from that in a slice cut downward. It is fascinating to see what patterns emerge when a slice of turnip or carrot is placed under a magnifying glass. With the aid of scientific equipment the process can be taken further and the whole structure of matter photographed magnifying to hundreds of times its normal size. The designs revealed this way are highly contemporary in feeling, as this kind of photography has only been possible in recent years, and these particular shapes are, therefore, symbolic of the age in which we live. Designs based on cellular structure, etc. are to be found in advertising, on wall-papers and fabrics and are the modern equivalent of the ubiquitous flowers and beasts of Elizabethan days. It must be stressed that any subject for design, however interesting, if used too often becomes a cliché and loses much of its impact.

Abstract Patterns

It is sometimes assumed by the layman that those who cannot draw, produce abstracts. In fact, all shapes are drawn, an abstract shape no less than a figurative one, and to make a good abstract design, both balanced and interesting is not easy. For one thing there is not the interest of subject matter to distract the viewer, and success depends solely on the components of the design itself, the arrangement of shapes, colours, etc. The onlooker is inclined, if he likes the subject of a design, to overlook some of its underlying formal qualities, but an abstract stands or falls by the merit of its design.

An abstract design can be based on geometric shapes, i.e. shapes which can be drawn with mathematical instruments, circles, hexagons, triangles, etc.; on freely drawn organic shapes; or on accidental effects such as blots, dribbles of paint, etc. Some designs based on geometric shapes are rather stiff and formal but can be very dignified and impressive in the right context. Geometric shapes invested with a symbolic meaning take on a different character and can evoke powerful emotions. Often, however, more vigour and vitality is to be found in designs based on freely drawn shapes.

It has been seen that when making a figurative design there is a definite starting-off point, namely the subject, which then has to be translated into a suitable flat pattern. With purely abstract designs, i.e. those that have no figurative subject matter, the designer is sometimes at a loss to know how to begin. Here are some suggestions how ideas might be initiated.

1. *Cutting Paper*. When working out designs in cut paper it is advisable to use paper of a dark tone for cutting out and white paper as a background or vice versa. In this way the cut shapes and intervening spaces show up strongly and faults in the design are made more obvious. This does not mean that the ensuing piece of embroidery must be interpreted in the same tonal relationship. It is merely a way of emphasizing the structure of the design at the planning stage. For those with definite ideas, cutting paper is just another way of drawing, a way of making shapes which can easily be translated into embroidery. For the more hesitant, a definite starting point might be useful, such as "exploding" a circle or square (Figs. 17 (*top two*)). The original figure is cut across with a razor blade in several places and the resulting pieces moved outward and arranged in a satisfactory design. Border designs can be made by simply cutting up a strip of paper in unequal sections and spacing the pieces out (Fig. 17 (*bottom*)). A slightly more complicated scheme is to cut several shapes out inside the edge of square or rectangle (or indeed any other shape) and fold each one over on the edge of the original figure (Fig. 17 (*centre, left*)). A further experiment could be to cut several shapes out of the centre of a figure and arrange them in any satisfying order round the edge (Fig. 17 (*centre, right*)). More subtle designs can be evolved by using transparent or semi-transparent papers and overlapping shapes to produce secondary shapes and colours where the overlapping takes place. Once a start is made one idea leads to another. If the best of the resulting designs are kept in a note book or filed away, a useful "pool" of ideas will soon be built up to be referred to when needed.

2. *Ink Blots and Dribbled Paint*. These methods are not as haphazard as they would at first seem as the hand is guided

Fig. 17.   Designing with Cut Paper
Top row, left: "Exploded" circle, and *right,* square
Middle row, left: Shapes cut from a rectangle and folded outwards on the edge.   *Right:* Pieces cut from an irregular figure and rearranged round the original shape
Bottom row: Long strip exploded

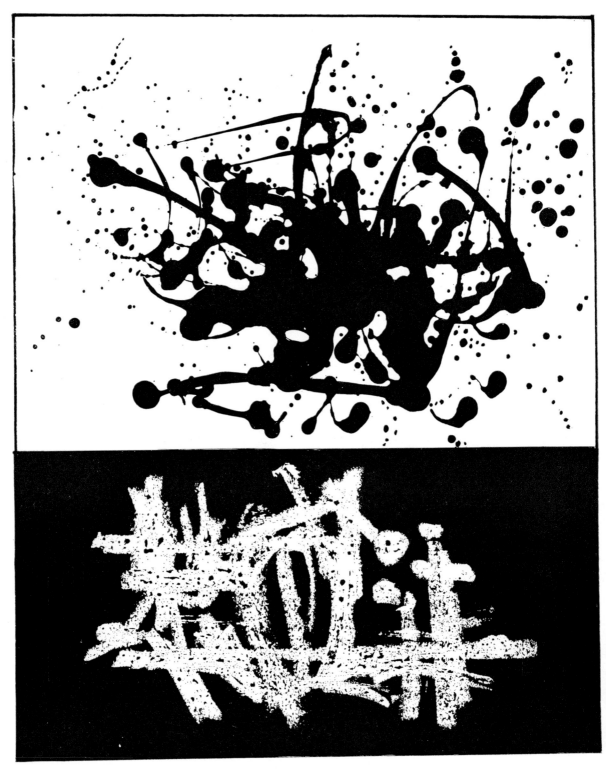

Fig. 18.   *Upper:* Paint Splashed on to Paper from a Height
            Lower: Indian Ink run over Paper Previously Rubbed with Candle

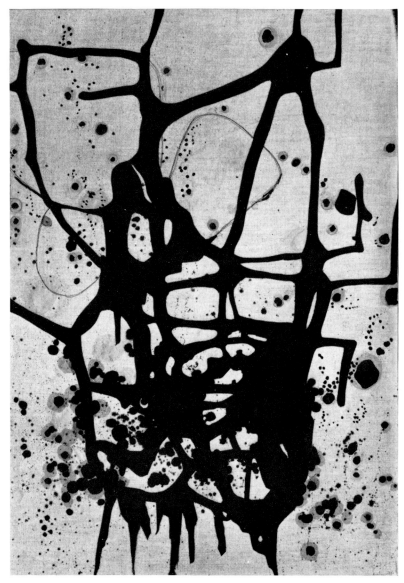

8. INTERPRETATION IN HESSIAN, FELT AND NET OF AN INK BLOT DESIGN. The design was made by placing a small pool of ink on to a sheet of paper and tipping the paper in different directions. Further details were added with ink splattered from a brush. The panel was designed and worked by Kathleen Wilmott, a student at Hornsey College of Art

to a great extent by one's intuitive sense of design. The design may not be consciously planned but nevertheless it cannot be called completely accidental. (As long ago as the Italian Renaissance Leonardo Da Vinci recommended throwing a paint-laden sponge against the wall to see what sort of pattern would emerge!) A blot may be made and the paper

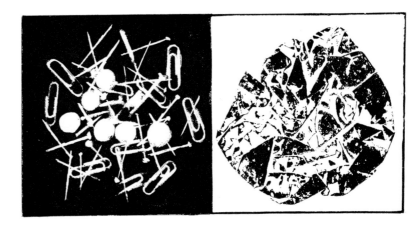

Fig. 19 (*right*). *Left,* Drawing Pins, Paper Clips, etc., Placed on Paper and Sprayed with Aerosol Paint, Voiding the Design
Right, Print Taken from a Crumpled Sheet of Paper

Fig. 20 (*below*). Small Object Revolved between Strong Light and Paper, and the cast Shadow "Filled in". Four Positions are Shown out of an Infinite Number of Possible ones

folded or crumpled up, alternatively, a small pool of ink may be placed in the centre of a piece of paper and the paper tipped this way and that until an interesting pattern is built up. The design for the panel in Plate 8 was carried out in this way. Additions can be made with brush or pen. Paint can be dribbled on to paper from an overloaded brush or washed over a surface previously rubbed with wax. Again further ideas will occur as the experiment progresses (Fig. 18).

3. Rubbing. If a piece of paper is placed over a textured surface and rubbed with a soft pencil, crayon or cobbler's heel-ball (as used for brass rubbings) the pattern of the surface will emerge. A more interesting pattern will be made if the surface chosen has definite points of interest (e.g. knot holes in a piece of wood).

4. Printing. Any textured or raised surface may be "inked up" and a print taken (Fig. 19 (*left*)). Conversely the pattern can be masked and the background filled in with a paint spray, voiding the design (Fig. 19 (*right*)).

5. Kaleidoscope. Symmetrical designs can be made with the aid of a kaleidoscope. Unlike the old-fashioned sort which had a permanent collection of coloured particles inside, the ones on the market today have a lens at the bottom end which can be trained on any object in sight. The variety and complexity of these designs is infinite.

6. Shadow Patterns. If any three dimensional object is suspended between a bright light and a sheet of white card or paper, and the object revolved, a series of patterns will be

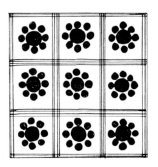

Fig. 21. Three Types of Regular Repeat. *Left*, Horizontal Rows. *Centre*, Half Drop. *Right*, Overlapping

made by the shadow of the object on the card. The shadows can actually be drawn round or filled in and later developed into suitable designs (Fig. 20).

7. *Slides.* Where there is a projector available, of the type used for showing colour transparencies, simple slides can be made to project on to the screen. Between two pieces of glass, seeds, small leaves, or bits of fabric can be mounted; anything, in fact, which is small enough and flat enough. Oil, coloured inks, paint or crayon can also be rubbed on to the glass. When these are projected, greatly magnified, on to the screen, unsuspected patterns will emerge.

Allover Patterns

There are times when allover pattern is preferable to a motif or group of motifs. An allover pattern in embroidery differs from one that is printed in that it does not necessarily have to repeat exactly. Even when the embroidered pattern is planned to repeat, a certain amount of variation will creep in in the working, unlike a printed design which is mechanically reproduced by a screen or block. It is this quality which gives a hand-made object its particular character, and differentiates it from the greater precision of mechanical repeats. This accounts for the lifelessness of patterns produced by an "automatic" embroidery machine. Free machine embroidery, however, is as creative as hand embroidery, the needle does what the embroiderer wants and does not follow a mechanically set pattern. Formal repeat patterns can be built up of geometric or organic shapes in a number of ways. Fig. 21 shows a motif (*left*) in horizontal and vertical rows,

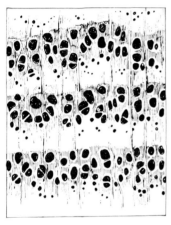

Fig. 22. Two Designs Taken
Direct from Nature which have
Unity without Repeating.
Upper, Cross-section of Agate.
Lower, Transverse Section of Tree

(*centre*) in a half drop, and (*right*) overlapping. The main structure of a pattern may be repeated but the details varied as in the Elizabethan cushion in Fig. 39. This gives a certain unity without monotony.

Even more interesting is the allover pattern which makes a unified design without actually repeating at all. Many such patterns are found in nature, e.g. the transverse sections of a tree and a piece of agate shown in Fig. 22. A pattern has been described as a series of relationships, and it is this relationship, the "family likeness" between one shape and another, which gives the design in Fig. 23 (*upper*) its unity, despite the fact that there is no repeat at all. An allover pattern can become monotonous if motifs of the same weight are used throughout. An accent or focal point here and there creates interest. This is why a counterchange pattern is only successful up to a point. A certain monotony is inevitable as the light and dark areas are of necessity equal (Fig. 24). An allover pattern can be made up of separate motifs or it can be a continuous "doodle" (Fig. 23 (*lower*)). The latter type of design is particularly suited to machine embroidery. Even in a close allover pattern, shape should be carefully considered otherwise the result is no more than a surface texture.

Technique

This "grammar" of design is intended to apply generally to all types of embroidery and fabric collage, but it will be found that certain techniques inevitably influence the choice of colour, tone and texture. For example, it would be foolish to use curved shapes in a design intended to be carried out in cross stitch or canvas work. The very nature of work on the counted thread is angular, and it is wrong to try and force it into uncharacteristic shapes. In the same way, lacy types of embroidery such as cut work, net darning, and pulled fabric need to be worked in self colour. Using contrasting colours completely destroys the lacy effect which is aimed at. An inlay based on a counterchange design, on the other hand, demands a contrast of colour or tone to give it point. Texture is to a great extent inherent in the technique; pulled fabric or bead embroidery must give a raised texture, shadow work or pattern darning a relatively smooth surface.

From this it can be seen that either (*a*) the design must fulfil the limitations set upon it by the chosen method of embroidery, or (*b*) the method of embroidery must be chosen to fit in with the design. The sequence will depend largely on the practical application of the piece of work. Canvas work, for instance, may be needed specifically for its hard-wearing qualities for a chair seat or stool top. The sensible approach in this case is to fit the design to the required technique. When planning work which is to go behind glass, on the other hand, the design can come first, and the method chosen in which that design can be most successfully executed.

The many and varied embroidery techniques should never be regarded as an end in themselves, but as a way in which a particular design can be executed in the most practical and satisfactory way. It must not be thought that there is any intrinsic value in a particular type of embroidery which makes it superior to any other method. Gold work, which in the *right* setting looks immensely rich and exciting, could in the *wrong* place merely look tawdry, and far inferior to a simple applied shape, for instance. A method should always be chosen for its value *in that particular context*.

It is also a mistake to think that even stitching is always a virtue. More exciting results can often be obtained by deliberately varying the size and spacing of stitches. Technique should not be in any way careless (i.e. loose threads, badly finished ends, etc.), but a studied variation in the working of a stitch can give greater interest and vigour than a line of perfect regularity. In machine embroidery, too, unusual effects can be achieved by deliberately altering the tensions, substituting thick threads for the normal machine embroidery cotton in the spool, sewing down gimps, braids, nubbly knitting wools, etc. There is a danger (especially amongst embroiderers with a wide knowledge of traditional methods) of keeping each type of embroidery in a separate category, of limiting bead work to beads, and cut work to cut holes, for instance. In fact the two methods can be combined with interesting and unusual results (Plate 6). Many experiments could be carried out along these lines trying, for instance, a mixture of padded embroidery and cut-away spaces, or smocking with beadwork instead of the usual smocking stitches.

It cannot be stressed too strongly that constant experiment

Fig. 23. *Upper*, Design which Does not Repeat but Has Unity Because of "Family Resemblance" of Shapes *Lower*, Continuous Doodle

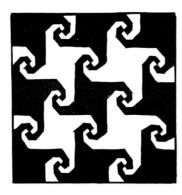

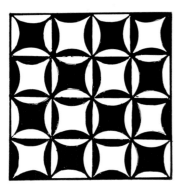

Fig. 24. Two Counterchange Designs Found in American Quilts The upper is called "Rob Peter to Pay Paul" a title which explains the principle of counterchange precisely

is essential in order to produce new and exciting ideas. In the past, embroiderers have not been afraid to try out unusual ideas such as stump work in the seventeenth century or string embroidery in the eighteenth century, and primitive people are adept at making use of available materials such as porcupine quills, seeds, leather, human and animal hair with successful results. On washable objects, of course, practicability is a somewhat limiting factor, but for anything mounted behind glass, or handled only occasionally, the possibilities for experimental techniques are endless. Some unconventional objects introduced successfully into embroidery and collage in recent years include melon seeds, date stones, wood and metal shavings, nuts, bolts, nails, tin lids, glass, buttons, pieces of tree bark.

The description of embroidery as a two-dimensional art form is sometimes wrongly interpreted as meaning that the surface should be flat. Nothing could be further from the truth. The term two-dimensional refers to the type of *design* most suitable for embroidery, *not to the actual surface of the work* (page 22). Indeed this three-dimensional quality of the surface of a piece of embroidery is one of its most interesting features, distinguishing it from dyes and printed patterns, which are essentially flat. This richness of surface texture can be exploited to the full by using raised stitches, padding, building up with layers of fabric, etc., or by cutting and folding the fabric in the manner of paper sculpture (Plates 3 and 24).

For pictures and panels experiments could be carried out in working on more than one level. For example, on to the front of a frame could be tacked a piece of transparent fabric, or one with holes cut in it through which could be seen a richly embroidered area on the second layer of fabric tacked on to the back of the frame. With a deep box frame it would be possible to have several inches depth between the two layers.

The possibilities are endless. Once the designer starts experimenting one idea leads to another and most exciting and unusual effects may be achieved. The important thing is to keep an open mind, being prepared to try anything interesting which is *within the bounds of practicability.*

Chapter Two

Embroidery on Dress

MAN seems to possess an instinctive desire to decorate his person, his clothes and his belongings. Anthropologists believe that clothes are worn primarily for their decorative value, and not, as might be supposed, for reasons of warmth or modesty. It is not surprising to find, therefore, that even when clothes were at their most primitive, no more than a few skins crudely sewn together, the leather thonging or grasses used to join them were laced together to form decorative patterns. From these simple beginnings has evolved a history of years of embroidery on dress.

Embroidery as we understand the term has been in existence for at least three thousand years. Although very few early pieces have survived, there is evidence from writings, sculpture and paintings that the peoples of the ancient civilizations (Egyptians, Babylonians, Persians and others) used embroidery extensively on their clothes. Their materials were wool, flax, cotton, and later, silk and gold. The gold was beaten out thinly and cut into strips and discs. The earliest surviving fragments are from Egyptian tombs and make use of simple stitches such as satin stitch and knots in linen thread on a linen ground. The Greeks were influenced by the Asian and Oriental embroideries which they imported, and oriental motifs such as the palmette were as popular as the indigenous Greek key pattern for borders on clothes. The Greeks influenced the Romans and also the Copts, the early Christians of Egypt, who produced beautiful embroidery, much of it on clothes. They used linen and wool, in rich sombre colours—reds, purples, blacks. A look at the mosaics of the time shows the sumptuousness of costume in Byzantium under the rule of Constantine in the

Fig. 25. Embroidered Borders Used on Costume
Top row: Minoan; English Nineteenth Century (machine embroidery); *Second row:* Egyptian; Spanish; *Third row:* Greek; Nineteenth-century French; *Bottom Row:* Roman; Anglo-Saxon

sixth century. Woven silks were embellished with rich all-over embroidery which incorporated pearls and rough-cut gem stones.

There is evidence that as early as the ninth century embroidery was used on dress in England. At first it was confined to borders on sleeves, necks and hems, with sometimes a band around the upper arm. Often jewels and metal discs (the forerunners of sequins) were incorporated. Later the return of warriors from the Crusades with girdles and pouches covered in Eastern embroidery created a demand for similar work in England. The twelfth century saw the birth of Heraldry. The flat areas of clear colour and stylized decorative motifs lent themselves particularly well to being interpreted in embroidery, and the women of medieval England decorated their mantles and cotehardies with their husbands' arms.

Whereas in medieval dress the embroidery was confined mainly to borders, girdles and accessories, by the sixteenth century it was used over the entire garment. During the reign of Elizabeth, even fabrics rich in themselves were embroidered all over in coloured silks, metal threads and jewels.

Women's skirts were worn open at the front to show elaborate petticoats underneath, and all accessories, such as shoes, gloves, collars, cuffs, and purses were embroidered. The introduction of the steel needle made finer work possible and black work consisting of minute filling stitches in black silk thread was particularly popular. Cut work, which later developed into needlepoint lace, was used for collars, cuffs, and edgings of gloves and handkerchiefs. The most typical embroidery design was an allover pattern of coiling stems enclosing flat formalized flowers. It was carried out in polychrome or monochrome, often with the addition of metal threads. This general use of embroidery on clothes continued into the first part of the seventeenth century without much change.

In the eighteenth century men's clothes outshone those of women in the richness of their embroidery. Coats and long waistcoats were embroidered to match, with rich floral designs in silks or metal threads. Men's evening coats glittered with tinsel and spangles and were sometimes even studded with diamonds. The women wore petticoats worked with quilting or pulled fabric, and yellow or cream silk aprons decorated with fine silk flower embroidery reflecting the contemporary popularity of Chinoiserie. By the end of the century the so-called revival of Greek clothes and the vogue for white muslin for dresses and accessories brought Ayrshire embroidery to the fore. This delicate embroidery with its contrasts of cut work, eyelets, fine needlepoint fillings, French knots and satin stitch, remained popular for accessories as well as for children's clothes through the first half of the nineteenth century. It was eventually superseded by the coarser Broderie Anglaise, and finally machine embroidery. Another type of white work used for accessories and children's clothes was Richelieu work, an elaborate form of cut work. In the 1880s smocking, which had previously been used only on working-men's shifts, became high fashion and was used on tennis dresses, tea gowns, jackets, blouses and on children's clothes for both boys and girls. During the latter part of the century, although surface embroidery as such was not much used on outer garments, great use was made of beading (particularly with jet), braids, ribbons, fringing and other decorative treatments.

Unlike most European countries, England has no tradition

Fig. 26. Eighteenth-century Child's Cap with Quilted Design

Fig. 27.   Pearly King's Suit and Waistcoat

of peasant embroidery. Whereas on the continent the poorest families found time to embroider elaborate trousseaux, costumes for special occasions, and even garments to be buried in, in England embroidery has remained, on the whole, the prerogative of the leisured classes. One exception is the smock, already mentioned, which was worn by the country worker in the latter part of the eighteenth and throughout the nineteenth century. It developed from the workman's shift which went back to Anglo-Saxon times, but it was not until the middle of the eighteenth century that the fullness was held together by the decorative means now known as "smocking." In addition to the actual smocking, panels on either side of the yoke were worked in feather stitch in designs depicting the wearer's trade. The smocks were almost always worked in linen thread on linen or twill, the colours, white, natural, blue or olive green, varying from county to county.

A more recent tradition in dress which could be classed as folk art is that of the pearly kings and queens who have reigned over their individual districts of London since the 1890s. Most pearly kings and queens design and make their own costumes, the decoration being made up entirely of pearl buttons sewn on the fabric of the suit or dress. An elaborately patterned suit can weigh up to twenty pounds in buttons, and the designs have great richness combined with originality and a naïve simplicity (Fig. 27).

In the twentieth century embroidery on dress has been confined mainly to ceremonial and evening wear. Apart from minor passing fashions, embroidery has not been a feature of everyday clothes. In the late sixties, however, there was something of a revolution in fashion, especially among the young, and clothes which a few years ago would have been considered fancy dress are now acceptable wear for men and women. Two reasons suggest themselves. One, that clothes are only echoing the theme of Fantasy which has now permeated posters, magazine illustration, advertising, the decoration of shops and boutiques, etc. Two, now that copies of Haute Couture clothes are rushed into the shops, at reasonable prices, within days of the Collections being shown, much of the mystique and reverence surrounding couture clothes has died. The new status symbols are the "one-off" models, that is, garments that are individually made and decorated in a way which would make mass production impracticable. Thus the beautiful, possibly fantastic, hand-embroidered garment comes into its own. Because of this, peasant clothes from Europe and the East, which a few years ago would have been considered "arty-crafty," are now high fashion. It is this kind of right-about-face which makes it essential for anyone interested in embroidering clothes to keep an open mind and be prepared to reappraise periodically what is "right" and fashionable for that particular time. Every period has its particular flavour (evolved from past fashion and prevailing social conditions) which is epitomized in its architecture, furniture, painting, sculpture, as well as in its clothes. The motif in Fig. 28 could only have been embroidered with any success

Fig. 28 Embroidered Motif on an Art Nouveau Dress Designed by Henry Van de Velde in 1898

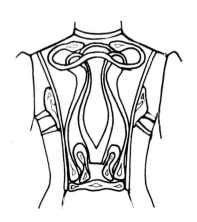

on a dress in the Art Nouveau period at the end of the nineteenth century. The same flowing curves were to be found in the contemporary furniture, ornaments, jewellery, posters, balustrades, etc. The embroidery design is successful because it fits into the climate of fashion prevailing at the time. The same design would have been unthinkable on say an Empire dress of seventy years earlier.

Good embroidery should be planned from the beginning as part of the design of the garment itself. There should be no feeling that the embroidery is an afterthought. If the embroidery is not an essential part of the whole, i.e. if the dress or blouse would be just as successful without the embroidery, then it is better omitted. Certain types of embroidery actually play a functional role in the make up of the garment, like quilting which provides warmth, smocking which controls fullness, or faggoting by which pieces can be joined together decoratively. This kind of work must, of necessity, be treated as part of the design of the garment. It is when the embroidery is of a purely ornamental nature that its inclusion needs to be considered particularly carefully.

Many different types of embroidery are suitable for use on dress. The choice depends on the fabric from which the garment is made and the occasions on which it will be worn. Elaborate bead embroidery, for instance, would be unpractical and look out of place on an every-day dress. Below is a list of methods of embroidery which are suitable for dress, and suggestions for the type of garments to which they are suited.

English Quilting. This is a method of joining several layers of material together where warmth or padding is required. The design, which should be allover in character in order that the various layers should not slip, can be carried out in running stitch, back stitch, or on the machine. Nowadays synthetic waddings make garments easy to wash and quick to dry. It is suitable for evening coats and skirts, jerkins, housecoats and so on. (Fig. 29.)

Smocking. This is a method of providing fullness in a decorative manner. It originated in the loose shifts worn by country workers, but is nowadays usually found on finer clothes; lingerie, blouses, children's clothes and so on.

Fig. 29. Three Simple Designs for English Quilting

9. *Left:* Tie with Appliqué and Machine Embroidery. Designed and worked by Christine Risley. This is a good example of automatic machine embroidery used with taste and discretion.
Top, right: Evening Shoe with Applied Gold Kid and Embroidery. Designed and made by Anne Marie Stannard at Hornsey College of Art.
Bottom, right: Leather Shoe with Embroidered Rosette. Designed and made by Cherstin Ohlson at Hornsey College of Art

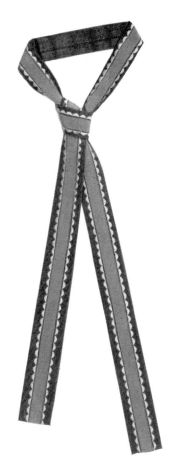

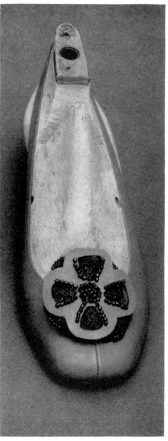

Fig. 30. Bead Embroidery
Top row: left, Border; *centre*, Motif voided on a beaded background; *right*, Two geometric motifs.
Bottom row: left, Stylized Flower Head; *right*, All-over pattern

Traditionally worked in rigid geometric patterns, it can be worked in a freer fashion, giving more interesting results. It looks best worked in restrained colour, possibly self colour, or one contrasting colour. If honeycombing is used on say a wedding dress, a small pearl or glass bead may be sewn on to it at each intersection.

Faggoting. This covers a number of different stitches and is a method of making open seams. It is especially suitable for fine materials and is used in lingerie, children's clothes and blouses.

Beading (Fig. 30). Beads are amongst the oldest of ornaments. In primitive times almost any thing with a hole in it served as a bead. Nuts, shells, seeds, stones, clay, metal, glass, bones, teeth and ivory have all been used. Today there is a wide range of beads and sequins on the market, made mainly of glass and synthetic substances. The term bead embroidery usually implies a decoration consisting entirely of beads sewn on to a fabric, but interesting results can be obtained by combining them with appliqué or surface stitches worked by hand or on the machine. Because of its ornate appearance, the impracticability of laundering, the expense and the time taken to execute the work, bead embroidery is usually confined to "special occasion" clothes. The shapes of beads are so varied and interesting that designs can be built up directly with the beads, rather than from drawings. Beads are heavy, so if flimsy fabrics are used they must be backed with muslin or lawn to support the weight of the beads. The edges of beads are sharp, making it advisable to use a strong pure silk thread for sewing them on. It is also a useful precaution to put a spot of rubber solution on to the endings of threads on the back of the work to prevent ends working loose and beads falling off. All bead embroidery should be worked before the garment is made up. In this way it can be put in a frame to keep it taut, and if even then distortion does occur it can be damped and stretched back into its true shape. If pressing is required after the garment is made up it should be done from the back of the work into a thick folded blanket.

Buttons. These can be used in much the same way as beads

10. PEASANT DRESS NOW USED FOR PARTY WEAR. The embroidery, which is in a mixture of Middle Eastern styles, is in silk and metal threads on a black homespun fabric. The dress itself is simple in design and crudely sewn together, but the embroidery is rich in pattern, colour and texture. Loaned by Sally Scott. *Below:* Detail of sleeve.

Fig. 31. Buttons Incorporated into a Design of Italian Quilting

Fig. 32. Allover Pattern Suitable for Italian Quilting
For this type of work the design must be built up with parallel rows of stitching

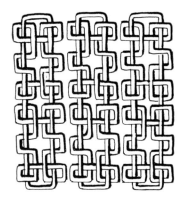

to build up a pattern or they can themselves be embroidered to form an important focus on a plain garment. Where surface embroidery is worked on an area which includes buttonholes, then the buttons can form part of the design (Fig. 31).

Appliqué. This is most suitable where bold simple shapes are required, or as a background to linear work such as machine embroidery which on its own can look rather thin. It can also be used on delicate materials for children's clothes, underwear, etc. Certain technical rules must be obeyed. For washable garments like materials must be used and the grain of the applied patches must correspond with that of the ground material. Edges must be turned in (which demands simple shapes) or covered with overcasting or satin stitch worked on the machine or by hand. Bold appliqué shapes can be used effectively on all play clothes, either left plain or enriched with surface stitchery in thick threads. For children's party dresses organdie on net or self-fabric makes a good basis for added embroidery. For evening clothes, gold or silver kid would combine well with metal threads.

Italian Quilting, Trapunto. These two types of quilting, unlike English quilting, do not perform a function but are purely decorative. Both are worked through a double layer of material. In Italian quilting the design is worked entirely in parallel lines of running or back stitch, which are then padded by inserting a thick wool from the back (Fig. 32). In the case of Trapunto, areas of the design are padded where required by splitting the backing and inserting wadding, after which the backing is sewn up again. Both types of embroidery can be successfully combined in one piece of work.

Broderie Anglaise. In Broderie Anglaise, which like cut work also makes use of holes, the holes are cut or pierced first, then the edges overcast. Broderie Anglaise is worked on fine linen or cotton, and is suitable for lingerie, blouses, children's and babies' clothes and trimmings (Fig. 33).

Cut Work. This can be carried out by hand or machine on any firmly woven fabric. It looks attractive on linen dresses, but is best confined to neck, sleeves or pockets where it would not need to be lined. The arrangement of the cut-

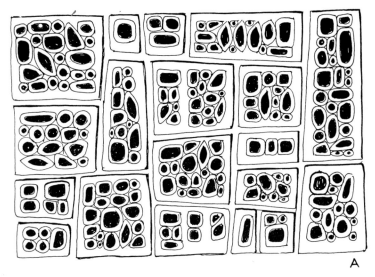

Fig. 33. Broderie Anglaise as (A) an Allover Pattern; (B) an Asymmetric motif; (C) A Formal Motif

Fig. 34. Cut Work which could be Used on a Pocket or Repeated as an Allover Pattern

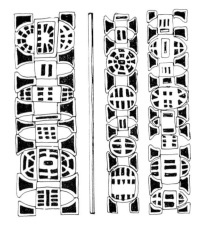

away areas should be carefully considered as they form the most important part of the design. The entire design is worked in buttonhole stitch before any material is cut away (Fig. 34).

Drawn Thread Work. This also gives open spaces, but as it involves withdrawing warp or weft threads design is limited to simple vertical and horizontal arrangements (Fig. 35).

Needleweaving. This is a variation of drawn thread work which could be used effectively on accessories such as handbags and belts (Plate 5).

Pulled work. For this holes are made without withdrawing threads from the ground fabric, but, as the name implies, by pulling and distorting the weave. There are dozens of different stitches, some giving very open effects, some only slightly altering the surface texture of the fabric. It is essential to use loosely woven materials or fine ones where the threads "give" easily.

Fig. 35. Drawn Thread Work must Follow the Horizontal and Vertical Direction of the Warp and Weft

Net embroidery. Whether in the hand or machine version, this gives a lace-like effect. It is suitable for use on stoles, handkerchiefs, etc., and can be inset into muslin, organdie, crêpe de chine, silk and so on, for underwear and children's party dresses (Plates 4 and 5).

Surface stitches. Surface stitches of all kinds can be used on dress, whether on their own or combined with any of the above methods. Where self colour is used, threads need to be bold and textures interesting. Where contrasting threads are used the embroidery can afford to be fine and flatter in character, for instance, black work. Stitches must be kept close so that they do not get caught up in things. Experiments should be made with unusual threads. Synthetic raffia, for instance, is ideal for summer clothes, play clothes and accessories. Gold and silver threads couched by hand, or synthetic metal threads (Lurex) used on the machine, are suitable for clothes and accessories for occasional use. Also suitable for couching are braids (from which elaborate patterns can be evolved), ribbons, and cords. The latter can be bought or made by hand. These are particularly suitable where a bold effect is required without too much time being expended.

The close texture and hard-wearing qualities of *machine embroidery* make it particularly suitable for embroidery on dress. Anyone attending classes at an art school will probably have access to trade machines on which chain stitch and

11. *Upper:* Front and Back View of Waistcoat. Designed and machine embroidered by Pat Phillpott. Both free machining and automatic stitches are used. *Lower:* Detail of Dress Embroidery by Pat Phillpott. Tucking is combined with automatic machine stitches and free whip stitch.

12. EMBROIDERED TROUSERS. Designed and worked by Sue Kemp for her husband. The design is a free "scribble" on the domestic machine, and could be adapted to suit almost any garment

a free satin stitch can be worked (the Cornely and the Irish Machines), but even on a simple straight-stitching domestic machine a wide variety of effects may be obtained. The only essential condition is that the machine must be electrified or worked by a treadle, as the hands must be left free. Several books are mentioned on page 123 which explain clearly how to adapt the machine to work embroidery. The rest is a matter of practice to attain practical skill.

Machine embroidery varies greatly in character from most hand embroidery. It is, generally speaking, close in texture and is worked continuously rather than in isolated units. Because the working method is so akin to drawing there is a tendency to produce line drawings which might just as well have been done with a pencil. For this reason it is doubly important to keep in mind the intrinsic qualities of good embroidery design. Monotony of texture can be overcome by

13. DRESS AND COAT FOR A SMALL GIRL
The dress uses grey and white and black and white gingham, the poplin coat trimmed with braid is reversible. Designed and made by Jane Macklin at the Rachel McMillan Training College

using satin stitch, whip stitch and cable stitch; by combining the machine embroidery with beads or surface stitches worked by hand; or by incorporating cut work where it is suitable. The rather thin linear quality of much machine embroidery can be counteracted by machining over solid areas of appliqué which give weight to the design. The machine is also very useful for sewing down braids, ribbons, etc.

Any embroidery on dress should be worked where possible before the garment is made up. The entire pattern of the garment should be trace-tacked on to the fabric and the embroidery design transferred in the appropriate places. This makes it possible to frame up the sections if necessary, as it would be, for instance, to work bead embroidery or quilting.

Colour and tone should be carefully considered when designing embroidery for dress. Strongly contrasting tones

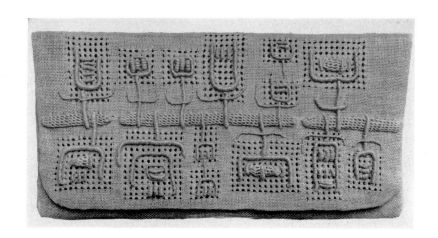

14. Two Handbags for Everyday
Use. The top one, in Casalguidi
embroidery, designed by Eirian
Short for the Embroiderers' Guild
and worked by Mrs. Nancy
Kimmins. The bag in mattress tick-
ing decorated with braids was
designed and worked by Judith
Porritt at the Rachel McMillan
Training College

make the embroidery stand out, close tones give a subtle effect. It must be decided which effect is required in each particular case. It is good to think afresh and get away from clichés. Children's clothes, for instance, need not be made in clear, bright primary colours, or pastels. A small girl can look wonderful in sombre colours or dark tones. Similarly, lingerie in navy or dark brown can be more interesting than the more usual white and flesh colours. Beach clothes can take bold areas of really "jazzy" colours, as bright sunlight takes much of the colour out. Play clothes generally can be given a bold, gay treatment—it is in the clothes worn for everyday that more restraint is needed.

Accessories of all sorts lend themselves to embroidered decoration, and can be attempted by those who find the making up of garments beyond their capabilities. Here are some suggestions—

Belts, for everyday wear in suède or leather with leather appliqué and simple machine stitching, for evening thickly encrusted with jet beads to wear with a plain dinner dress in jersey or crêpe.

Handbags, for evening, glittering with metal threads, beads, gold or silver kid; for day in linen with chunky, self-colour embroidery. (Plates 14 and 15.)

Collars and cuffs in any lacy open embroidery, net darning, Broderie Anglaise, cut work or in shadow work.

Evening shoes in satin or silk with silk embroidery and possibly imitation gemstones: slippers in soft leather, felt or fabric.

White cotton stockings for girls embroidered in self colour, or with coloured "clocks."

Gloves, with simple self-colour embroidery round the cuffs on the backs for day wear; elbow length with more elaborate decoration for evening wear or weddings.

Accessories can be made to tie up in design with one particular garment, or have an unobtrusive design which would

15. *Upper:* Bride's Handbag. Designed and worked by Anne Preston; *Lower: Left:* Shirt Front. Gingham of three different-sized squares is used, the smallest to cover the buttons; *Centre:* Buttons. Top to bottom—machine embroidery with added beads, hand embroidery, gold kid appliqué with machine embroidery and beads, whip stitch (machine), hand embroidery; *Right: top:* Beads; *bottom:* Couched String

enable them to fit in with many different outfits. It is important to study the practical aspect, as many accessories get hard wear (shoes, handbags) or are frequently washed (collars, light-coloured gloves).

The point made earlier about embroidery on dress being allied to fashion is equally true of embroidered accessories. An exquisitely embroidered collar will not contribute anything to a dress if at that time collars are not fashionable. On the other hand, an embroidered accessory which *is* in tune with the prevailing fashion can transform an everyday garment into one suitable for a special occasion.

Fig. 36. This Motif, based on a Persian Ceramic Design, could be Embroidered in Machine Embroidery or in Surface Stitchery by Hand

Chapter Three

Embroidery on Household Articles

M A N 's instinct to decorate his person and his clothes extends also to his home and its contents. Even nomads who have no fixed home go to great lengths to decorate the simple necessities of life which they carry around with them from place to place. A people who did this superbly were the Scythians. They inhabited the Steppes of Russia two thousand years ago and travelled from place to place in ox-drawn waggons which served as their homes when stationary. Their work was vigorous and powerful, combining acute observation of nature with a highly developed sense of decoration and their influence is clearly seen in the work of the Chinese and Northern European peoples. Details from two carpets of this period are shown in Figs. 37 and 38. As in almost all Scythian work, the designs of the two carpets are based on animal forms. By choosing as a basis for their designs the subject they knew best, they were able to produce highly formalized, decorative work without losing any of the power inherent in the subject. While fitting a stylized animal motif into a required shape, they at the same time were able to convey the pose and to capture the muscular strength of the animal concerned. The first detail is of a reindeer being attacked by a wild boar. The group is one of a series worked round the border of the carpet, the centre being quilted in an allover scrolling pattern. The animals are worked in a combination of appliqué and quilting, the quilting having a practical purpose as the carpet was probably used as a cover as well. The quilting although primarily functional, has been designed in such a way that it suggests the texture of skin and, by the direction of the stitches, heightens the sense of movement in the struggling beasts.

Fig. 37.   Detail of Scythian Quilted Carpet, First Century B.C. to Second Century A.D.

Appliqué is one of the oldest forms of embroidery, springing from the purely utilitarian patch.   It is not surprising therefore to find it used by nomadic tribes.   In this example the patches have been edged with cord, again fulfilling a double purpose, that of making the work more hard-wearing and emphasizing the animal forms.   The second detail shows a mythical beast, the dragon.   The entire carpet from which it is taken is worked in chain stitch, but there is no feeling of monotony.   It cannot be emphasized too strongly that it is not always necessary to use many different stitches to obtain

Fig. 38.   Detail of Scythian Carpet Worked Entirely in Chain Stitch

Fig. 39. Late Sixteenth-century Cushion, Satin Stitch and Couching on Red Satin

a lively and interesting effect. To use many different stitches *without good reason* results in muddle. A stitch should be used because it is the most satisfactory in that particular context, and for no other reason.

In Elizabethan England, when furniture was not upholstered, cushions played an important part in the furnishing of a room, being laid on chairs, benches, stools and window seats. Fig. 39 shows a red satin cushion of this period which has survived in excellent condition and may be seen at the Victoria and Albert Museum. The design is based on a simple structure, that of arabesques (S-shaped curves) spaced in such a way as to form enclosed heart shapes, and leaving no awkward spaces. In alternate rows the hearts are inverted making the design equally satisfactory when viewed from any angle. This non-directional type of design is important in an article which may be carelessly

thrown down and is, therefore, not always seen from the
same viewpoint. Designs which have a definite top and
bottom to them should be reserved for objects which are
normally seen in one position, such as fire screens, chair-
backs, finger-plates. Although the basis of the design is a
simple repeat, monotony has been avoided by varying the
motifs within the basic heart shape. Each flower or plant is
different, but because of its similarity of scale and treatment a
unity has been preserved. This happy combination of basic
simplicity with interesting permutations can form the basis
of many successful designs. Cushions played an important
part when furniture was not upholstered. Similarly, in the
days when houses were draughty and badly heated, much
attention was given to making the bed as cosy as possible.
In museums and country houses there is a wealth of embroidered bed furnishings in the form of quilts, coverlets,
curtains and valances. One particularly beautiful example
is the coverlet worked in Sicily around 1400 A.D. (Plate 16)
now owned by the Victoria and Albert Museum. This
design is an interesting example of a pictorial subject used to
enhance an everyday object, not an easy thing to do successfully. It is all too easy for such a design to look like a picture
stuck on and not a considered design. The coverlet tells the
story of Tristan, in a series of scenes showing different
incidents, in the manner of a strip cartoon. The secret of
success is that although incidentally telling the story graphic-
ally, it is primarily a design planned to fulfil a particular
function. Appropriately, the design is arranged to be
viewed from the bottom and sides, the usual angles from
which a bed is approached. The main motifs of figures,
ships, and buildings are grouped in a balanced but far from
static arrangement, and counterbalanced by the relatively
small scale pattern of lettering. Divisions between the
scenes are made in the border by free coiling plants, and in
the centre panel by a stiffer, formal arrangement of flower-
heads in rows. The quilt is worked in one colour so that the
highly padded embroidery is particularly effective in emphasizing the forms by the use of light and shade.

The Victoria and Albert Museum also owns the beautiful
crewel-work bed curtains embroidered in the seventeenth
century by Abigail Pett, a detail of which is shown in Fig. 40.
The design is one of scattered motifs in irregular rows, all the

16. PADDED LINEN BED-COVER, TELLING THE STORY OF TRISTAN.   Sicilian, *circa* 1400 A.D. (*By courtesy of the Victoria and Albert Museum*)

Fig. 40.   Detail of the Abigail Pett Bed-hangings in the Victoria and Albert Museum.
Second half of the Seventeenth Century

motifs being repeated more than once but never identically.
Variety is given each time by a slight change in design, a
different combination of filling stitches, different juxta-
position of colours.   The trees show the influence of Indian
cottons imported in the seventeenth century.   Some of the
animals too are exotic, the camel, the lion, the leopard,
monkeys in a bush; but others, the stag and the squirrel, are
taken from the English countryside.   Very English also is
the Morris dancer, one of the figure subjects which include a
man with a gun, another with a flag, and a fisherman fishing
in a naïvely drawn pool.   It might be thought that with such
a mixture the result would be a hotchpotch, but this is not the

case at all. The dynamic arrangement of the motifs in relation to one another, the clear, fresh colours, the variety in the filling stitches without losing a basic unity, the charming drawing of the individual motifs, all these combine to make one of the liveliest embroidery exhibits in the museum.

These few examples have been taken from the embroidery of the past because each one has a point to make which can help the designer today. In each case the design is related to the function of the object and consequently the view from which that object is normally seen. Also the character of the design relates to the type of embroidery used. In the Sicilian quilt, for example, the design is broken up into small enclosed areas suitable for padding, in the Scythian carpet the applied shapes are large and fairly simple. Quite an intricate design, on the other hand, is used on the cushion which is carried out in surface stitchery only. Last and quite important is the fact that each, though decorative in itself, sprang from a practical need at the time when it was made. In present-day furnishing also there is a feeling for function as well as decoration and there is certainly no place in the modern household for embroidered knick-knacks which clutter up the appearance of a room. Small mats, table runners, *Radio Times* covers are quite unnecessary and serve no better reason than to occupy someone for a few hours in the working of them. William Morris said, "Have nothing in your home which is not both beautiful and useful," and this applies just as much today as it did in his time. This does not mean that rooms today must be coldly clinical, but rather that embroidery should be used in a way which fits in with the present-day conception of combined usefulness and decoration. Many uses for embroidery will spring directly from the present-day way of life, as for instance, room-dividers from open-plan living, and attractive curtains and chair seats for the dining-kitchen.

When one embroidered article has been carried out in a room others can be made to link up with it in some way to preserve a certain unity. For example, a link up can be made between embroidery and some architectural feature of the room. In Fig. 41 (*upper*) the motif used as a repeat pattern on the tiled floor has been adapted and used on the lampshade and two cushion covers. In the same way a butterfly motif from the net room-divider in Fig. 41 (*lower*) could be repeated in a completely different medium, say a canvas-work stool-top or cushion-cover in another part of the room. A moulded plaster medallion on the ceiling could be translated into the design for a quilted cushion; or the continuous lines of a piece of wrought iron could form the basis of a design in Italian quilting or machine embroidery.

It is important from the beginning to think of the embroidery as an integral part of the decoration of the room, not to work the embroidery and then hope that it will fit in somewhere. From the beginning it should be planned in conjunction with the rest of the room, taking into consideration the colour scheme, the character of any existing pattern (abstract, floral, etc.), the embroidery's place in the setting and its practical use. Good interior designers sometimes go as far as having carpets specially designed and manufactured to fit into one particular room. This is obviously impossible for the average person, but any embroidered article can be specially designed to enhance, rather than confuse, the decoration. In a room with plain carpets and fabrics, with simple furnishings almost any richly-embroidered article would make an interesting focal point, but when wall papers, patterned fabrics and carpets are used any embroidery must be more carefully considered to avoid a "messy" effect. Any pattern present will probably have some distinct character, i.e. be geometric, floral, etc. This can be utilized in different ways. One way would be for the embroidery to carry on the same theme, and so where the curtains have a bold sunflower print, a round rug could be worked with one giant over-life-size sunflower as its basis. Alternatively in a room where geometric shapes only were used it could be more interesting to introduce a figurative element into the embroidery, while keeping the treatment simple and stylized to fit in with the general scheme. It is impossible to lay down definite rules, each room must be considered on its own merits, much depends on the character of the rest of the house, the type of life the occupier leads, and so on.

Planning the design for embroidery on household articles can be carried out in a logical series of steps, the starting-off point being the shape of the article itself. A tablecloth, for instance, could be round, square, rectangular, octagonal, made to fit the table top exactly, or to hang down at the sides. Once the main shape has been decided on, the

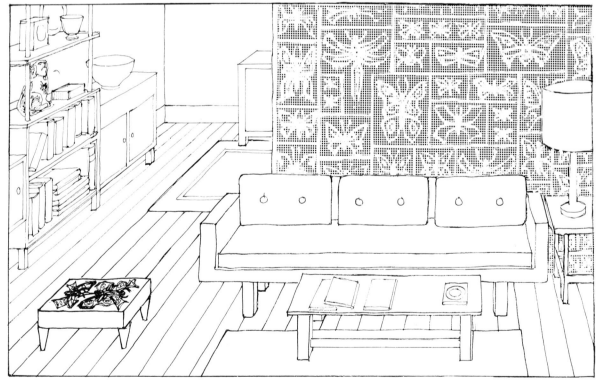

Fig. 41. *Top:* Motif from Tiled Floor Adapted for Embroidered Lampshade and Cushions
Bottom: Net Room-divider Linked in Design with Stool-top in Canvas Work

Fig. 42. Six Basic Arrangements for Tablecloth designs

embroidery must be planned in relation to that shape. At this point it is helpful to make a series of thumbnail sketches, showing a variety of possible arrangements. These drawings should be in no way detailed but should indicate the placing of the main areas of embroidery and their relative weights. The placing of the embroidery should be considered in relation to the function of the article. A tablecloth designed with the table setting in mind will enhance the general effect rather than confuse it. Of the six thumbnail sketches in Fig. 42 the most successful are those which leave the centre free, enabling the table to be set without looking cluttered. At this point, too, attention should be paid to the viewpoint from which the article will normally be viewed. On this will depend whether the design is non-directional or has a definite right and wrong way up (Fig. 43).

From this point on it is a matter of developing the design in more detail keeping in mind from the first the use to which the article is to be put, and the kind of materials in which the embroidery will be worked. The latter will decide the

Fig. 43. A Design with Definite Top and Bottom is shown above. In the lower illustrations the same motif has been used in a non-directional design

types of shapes used. For example if the medium chosen is machine embroidery, then a fairly intricate design with continuous lines would be suitable, whereas for appliqué, simple solid areas must play some part in the design. It must also be decided whether the effect aimed at is of a fairly static, formal quality or of a lively pattern; whether the design is to be based on a theme or subject, or whether it is to be abstract, and if it is abstract, whether geometric or organic in feeling (*see* Chapter I). It is a matter of personal choice whether the design is worked out in great detail on paper or whether only sufficient is indicated to enable the embroiderer to start work. Even if quite detailed work is done on paper it should not be assumed that drawing ends here. A line made with needle and thread on fabric is just as much a drawn line as one made with pencil on paper and the process of creating goes on until the last stitch is completed. This is one of the reasons why the mechanical filling in of a ready-made design is so unsatisfactory—there is no development as the practical work proceeds.

THE BED

The bed, symbolizing as it does, birth, marriage and death, has always been one of the most important items of furniture in the home. From ancient times beds have been painted, carved and hung with rich embroideries and have been the centre of many ceremonial and social occasions. Kings have held court in them, peasant brides have pushed them through the streets, piled high with embroidered pillows, witness to their industry in preparing for marriage. Although no longer the centrepiece of public ceremonies, the bed, by its symbolic significance, its size and position is still the dominating feature of the bedroom. It can take a bold and decorative treatment in the form of embroidered cover or bedhead. Curtains and valances are not usual today, although there are modern four-posters on which embroidered net or nylon curtains would look well. Three of the most popular forms of embroidery for bedcovers, namely quilting, patchwork and candlewick are those which flourished in the New World, the methods springing naturally from the social conditions of the time. Quilting made possible the use of old covers and blankets providing warmth without much out-

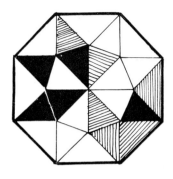

Fig. 44. The Importance of Tone in Patchwork Design
Top: Haphazard arrangement
Centre: Organized Symmetrical Arrangement
Bottom: Asymmetric but Balanced Design

lay on materials; patchwork enabled every precious scrap of fabric to be used up, in a country where new fabrics were hard to come by; and candlewick meant literally what it said, being worked from candle wicks, often the only thread available. The name candlewick has become somewhat debased because of its association with the ubiquitous commercially produced tufted bedspreads of the present day, but there is no reason why good designs should not be carried out in candlewick cotton, using either tufting or couching and surface stitchery.

Patchwork. As there is no way of mass-producing patchwork the reputation of this type of work has not suffered in the same way as that of candlewick, and a good patchwork quilt has a prestige value in keeping with the labour that goes into the making of it. A well-planned patchwork quilt with carefully selected scraps can look very striking. A visit to the quilt room at the American Museum in Bath is a breath-taking experience. The beauty of the minutely-printed fabrics, the simplicity and inventiveness of the individual motifs, combined with the richly-quilted surface texture, make a unique combination. In the realm of purely domestic embroidery, these patchwork quilts stand high. Their secret lies in the careful planning of the patches. Too many people use any old scraps, and put them together in a hap-hazard manner, the result being a confused jumble. Fabrics of a similar type should be selected: all cotton, all silk, all velvet, etc. (preferably cotton or linen) and the tonal quality in particular should be taken into account. Fig. 44 shows the same basic shapes arranged (*above*) with no regard to tone, and (*centre* and *below*) tonally considered. The results speak for themselves. Mosaic, or pieced patchwork (i.e. where the pieces are joined edge to edge) can be used for the entire cover; alternatively, patchwork motifs can be applied on to a plain cover. The latter method is much quicker, of course, and for a cover such as a child's which will frequently be washed, more hard wearing. Aluminium templates can be bought in a number of geometric shapes and also a shell pattern, but it is a simple matter to cut one's own out of a piece of stiff mounting card. A thick cartridge paper is suitable for the shapes to be covered. It is firm enough to work with and not too hard to tack through. When the patches

17. BED COVER IN PATCHWORK, APPLIQUÉ AND QUILTING. The patches are cottons in bright, clear colours. The white background is quilted in a simple diamond pattern. Mid-nineteenth century, Canandaigua, New York. (*By courtesy of the American Museum in Britain, Claverton Manor, Bath, Somerset*)

are prepared, they can be arranged on the bed and any necessary changes in design made before the pieces are sewn together. Patchwork can be used in conjunction with quilting, or with surface stitchery. Embroidery can be worked on some of the patches before tacking them on to paper, or used to cover the joins after the quilt is assembled. Quilting is worked after the patchwork is completed.

Fig. 45. Traditional Welsh Bed Quilt

Quilting. This on plain fabric or patchwork has the great advantage of combining function (warmth) with decoration. As the primary function of the embroidery is to hold the various layers of material together, the design must obviously be fairly evenly distributed. Apart from this consideration almost any type of design is suitable. Long continuous lines are less tedious to work than separate motifs but the two can be combined. If a change of texture or the introduction of a different colour is wanted, motifs in surface stitchery can be embroidered on the top layer of fabric before the layers are tacked together or after the quilting is finished. The earliest English quilts were made of linen and it remains one of the most effective materials for quilting. However, cottons, chintzes, etc., can be used successfully, but it is best to avoid very shiny fabrics such as satin which can look cheap.

English quilting usually consists of three layers, a backing, an interlining or padding, and the surface fabric. For reasons of economy, old blankets can be used for the padding, otherwise a synthetic interlining such as terylene wadding makes the quilt easy to launder. Ideally, the quilt should be worked on a large frame, but where this is impractical great care must be taken to ensure that all the layers are free of puckers and carefully tacked together before stitching begins. The layers of fabric can be laid out on a large table or on the floor and tacked outward from the middle to ensure this. The main lines of the design can be chalked in or tacked on to the top fabric, details being put in freely or drawn round a template depending on the type of design. Traditional quilt designs were usually built up with templates, being geometric in character, or based on leaves, feathers, shells, hearts, etc., according to the district in which they were worked. There is no reason why a traditional *method* of embroidery should necessarily be carried out in a traditional *design* and the present-day quilt should be in keeping with its surroundings, and bear the personal stamp of the designer. The design could be based on some personal feature, such as the trade or profession of the worker; a hobby such as angling, gardening, collecting, or it could feature details of the house itself or its environs. Alternatively, the design could be based on a purely abstract arrangement of shapes.

Appliqué. Appliqué, like patchwork, should be confined to materials of a similar type. Turnings are essential, so shapes should be simple, without sharp points. The design could be worked out by laying the ground fabric on the bed and arranging cut paper shapes until a satisfactory design is achieved. Any intricate linear work or details can be added in surface stitchery after the appliqué is completed.

When surface stitchery only is used for an article as large as a bed cover, the scale of the work needs to be constantly kept in mind. Fine stitchery is ineffective and a waste of time; bold results should be aimed at. In order to show up at distance and also to cover the ground quickly, braids, cords, ribbons, etc., can be incorporated into the work. These can be sewn down by hand or machine, with the addition of stitchery in thick threads such as perle, soft embroidery, cotton, etc.

Fitted but detachable covers for the bedhead are a practical idea. Quilting in particular would be suitable for this purpose. If some other method of embroidery is used, a separate padding could be made to go underneath (as in a teacosy).

There are on the market today some beautifully simple modern four-poster beds. Instead of the heavy curtains

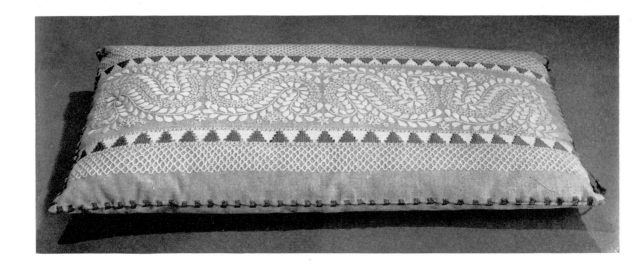

18. *Upper:* HUNGARIAN CUSHION COVER. (*In the Collection of the Embroiderers' Guild*) *Lower:* TABLE-MAT AND NAPKIN IN WHITE THREADS OF DIFFERENT THICKNESSES ON RED LINEN. A basically simple design which could be adapted to almost any article of household linen. Designed for The Embroiderers' Guild by Eirian Short

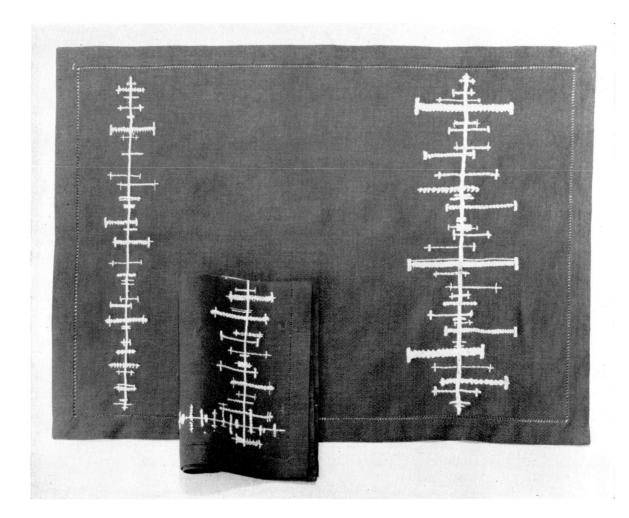

19. GINGHAM TABLECLOTH.
Designed and worked by Andrea
Potts at the Rachel McMillan
Training College. The gingham is
pieced and pleated to make an
unusual pattern. A detail of the
pleating is shown

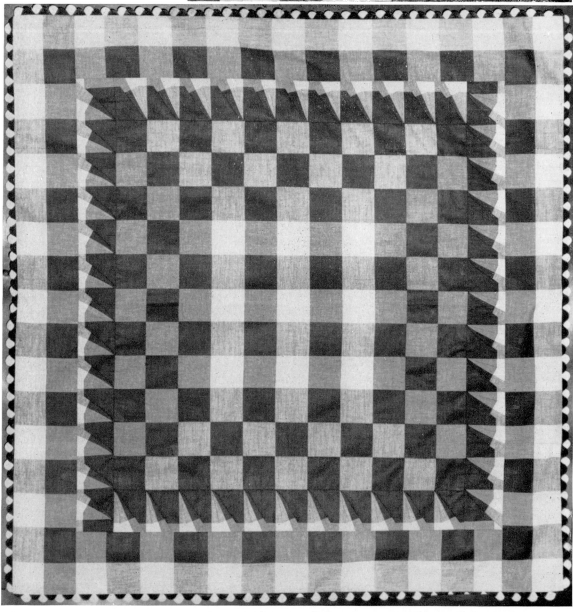

associated with the period four-poster, modern ones may have some light hangings in net, nylon or muslin. Machine embroidery in self-colour, net darning by hand, net insets on muslin, or nylon applied on to net would give a light airy effect in keeping with a present day bedroom.

If the bed cover has a bold design, any embroidery on the actual bed linen should be kept simple, possibly to self colour. Initials and monograms are particularly suitable but simple borders on pillow cases and sheet hems can also be effective. Close stitching is absolutely essential for anything laundered as often as bed linen. Machine embroidery for this reason is an obvious choice. If the work is in self colour, ordinary darning stitch would not show up. Satin stitch, where practicable or, if a straight-stitching domestic machine only is available, whip stitch would show up well. Alternatively satin stitch or any textured stitch could be worked by hand. Embroidery on pillows must obviously be confined to the edges. It would be most uncomfortable to lie on the embroidery. Pillow slips and sheets can be linked with a similar border pattern worked fairly boldly on the sheet but scaled down on the pillow. Contrasts in fabric can be used as a basis for the design, such as a plain white edging embroidered in self colour on a coloured sheet; striped or spotted fabric, with embroidered additions on a plain sheet, and so on. Initials could be designed as a separate motif or incorporated into a repeating design (Fig. 46).

TABLE LINEN

Another important focus in the home is the table. When the first oriental carpets were imported into this country by wealthy men in the sixteenth century, they were considered far too precious to be put on the floor and were used as table covers. In the sixteenth century too, great families worked their own table carpets in tent stitch on canvas sometimes incorporating their coats of arms into the design. Table covers as such are not in common use today, although a round table in a bedroom or drawing-room may sometimes have a floor-length cover permanently in position. The dining table, however, is usually laid for meals with a cloth or table-mats of some kind. Any washable fabric is suitable and can

Fig. 46. Lettering on Household Linen
Top row: Initial G in Broderie Anglaise. Borders based on H and Q
Middle row: Folded napkin. Initials incorporated into simple motifs
Bottom row: Initials enclosed in circular motif could be adapted for many purposes. Letters combined with formal embroidery on the counted thread

vary from a coarsely woven linen to delicate lawn or organdie. Much will depend on the general décor of the room, which meal the cloth is intended to be used at, the character of the china and cutlery, etc. The planning of the design is dealt with on pages 64 and 66. Some suggestions for suitable fabrics and appropriate embroidery are listed below.

A loose evenweave linen could be used for drawn-thread-work, arranged in bands or as a ground to emphasize a plain motif, also for pulled fabric, cross stitch, and Assisi work or open filling stitches on the counted thread. When using such traditional methods of embroidery an effort should be made to design imaginatively, in a personal way, rather than

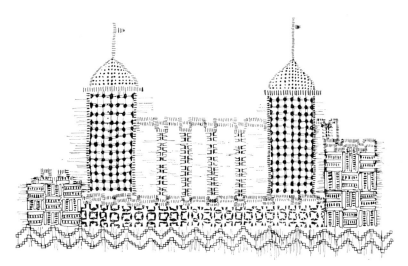

Fig. 47. Detail of pulled-work tablecloth based on London Buildings (*see* Plate 20 opposite)

to fall back on designs seen many times before. Plate 20 and Fig. 47 show details of a tablecloth worked in pulled fabric, depicting some of the famous buildings of London, and including the designer's own house. A little fresh thinking is all that is generally needed to get out of the usual rut. Black work, for instance, which is usually worked as a filling stitch within an outline, can look more interesting with the outline omitted and the stitch itself forming a lively silhouette. Organdie or lawn can look charming for an afternoon cloth. If organdie is used the hem may be folded double or even treble to give weight and make the cloth hang well. Appliqué in self fabric pinstitched in position could form a basis for the design. A closely-woven linen suggests cut work in self colour to give a lacy effect, surface stitchery, or a combination of the two. Dress linens and linen-type rayons are excellent for surface stitchery where an even weave is not required and have the advantage of coming in a far wider range of colours than embroidery linen. Strong, clear colours make an excellent ground for bold surface stitchery in contrasting colours and tones. Cotton tablecloths suitable for kitchen use can be quickly embroidered with a combination of appliqué and machine embroidery. The appliqué could include the sewing down on the machine of washable braids. Any long loose stitchery, large cut-away areas, etc., are out of place.

Most of the above suggestions apply equally to table mats.

20. *Upper:* TOWER BRIDGE. Detail of a tablecloth in pulled work, with a border of famous London buildings. The tablecloth which is over six feet in length, was designed and worked by Tecla Finck
Lower: PART OF A SAMPLER OF LETTERING. (*From the Collection of the Embroiderers' Guild*)

Planning the design is somewhat different in that a table mat can have a definite top and bottom to the design, it is not viewed from all sides as is a tablecloth. With place mats, which are big enough to take the complete setting, the embroidery can be confined to the ends where it will show when plates and cutlery are in position. Table mats can be made of single thickness, or envelope shaped to hold a heatproof mat. Napkins, tea cosies, etc., can be designed to link up with the tablecloth or mats. Napkins for family use, which are re-used, can usefully be decorated with some distinguishing mark such as an initial or symbol. Alternatively, the napkin can be worked with the same motif but in a different colour on each. The decoration on the napkin should be designed to look equally right when the napkin is folded or when it is opened out in use. Fig. 46 shows some suggestions for incorporating initials into the design.

CUSHIONS

Probably the most useful and versatile object in soft furnishings is the cushion. It is easily moved from place to place, can be used singly or massed with others, can be put on the floor when extra seating is needed, can transform a divan from a bed into an acceptable piece of living-room furniture. It can make a low seat high, a hard seat comfortable and generally speaking, it is difficult to have too many of them. Cushions from the embroiderer's point of view are ideal to design for. They can be made in a variety of shapes from a wide choice of fabrics, are of a manageable size for working, and do not take too long to carry out. It is often more encouraging for the beginner to work out two or three fairly quick pieces of work than to start on a large piece and get discouraged before it is finished. Because of their size, cushions can be made of inexpensive remnants.

Whatever the shape decided on for the cushion, the cover should be made separately so that it can be removed for washing or cleaning. The actual cushion can be made of mattress ticking filled with feathers, kapok or latex foam. All geometric shapes are suitable for cushions—squares, triangles, circles, ovals, diamonds, cylinders and the rest. There is nothing to stop one trying out simple organic shapes (e.g. kidney-shape) provided the result does not look fussy

21. TABLECLOTH WORKED BY IRISH NUNS IN THE NINETEENTH CENTURY. The detail shows a close-up of the three methods used, Drawn thread work, Ayrshire work and Tatting. (*By courtesy of the Embroiderers' Guild*)

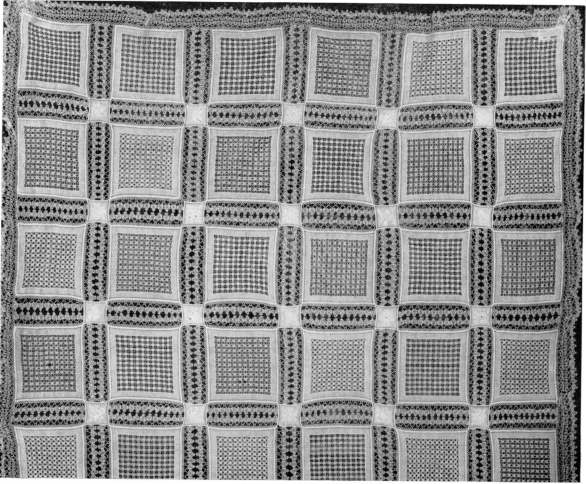

Fig. 48.   Front and back view of
Room-divider in Felt Inlay
Both designs are cut simultaneously
with a razor-blade and the cut pieces
interchanged

or contrived.   Cushions can vary in size from small scatter cushions about 12–15 inches across to a large pillow shape 27 by 16 inches.   Anything beyond this size becomes unwieldy.

Apart from tie-on cushions for dining chairs, all cushions should have a non-directional design.   The cover could have a motif on the front and back so that it can be thrown down either way up and still look satisfactory.   Embroidery for a cushion should be hard-wearing.   Canvas work, quilting, crewel work, tweed or flannel with felt appliqué would be suitable for a living room; cotton or linen for kitchen chair-seats, with appliqué in self fabric, machine embroidery or close surface stitchery.   For bedroom cushions finer fabrics and technique could be used as the cushions would not come in for much hard wear.   The embroidery could be carried out in Italian quilting, shadow quilting, surface embroidery or machine embroidery.

ROOM DIVIDERS

A feature of modern open-plan living-rooms is often the room divider, screening the dining area or study from the main sitting room.   An opaque divider such as a heavy curtain could be embroidered on either side.   Two hangings put back to back with a slightly stiffened interlining would be ideal.   The design on the second side could be a counter-change of the first side.   The material for the two sides could be cut out simultaneously by laying two different coloured felts one on top of the other and cutting out the shapes with a blade or cutting knife.   The cut-out pieces from the side shown above could then be inserted into the holes in the side below and vice versa (Fig. 48).   This, however, is only one suggestion. Any embroidery on a bold scale would be suitable.   If the curtain is to be pulled back at any time it would be better not to use felt but to chose a furnishing fabric which would hang in folds.   It may be that a *suggestion* of screening off is all that is required in which case a semi-transparent or com-pletely transparent curtain would give a feeling of light and space, and yet suggest a partition.   The ideal ground fabric for a curtain of this sort would be one of the many varieties of curtain-net on the market today.   They vary from a fine plain mesh, to heavy cotton "vision net" with a distinct decorative pattern.   On the latter, parts of the design could

Fig. 49.   Detail of Room-divider in Fig. 41

be emphasized by darning in thick cottons, etc., the former leaves the designer free to use any suitable motif and a variety of methods.   An airy feeling could be achieved, for example, by cutting away holes in the net, machining or over-casting the edges and then working fine "spider's webs" across the holes.   Net darning in a variety of different thick-nesses of thread was used for the curtains in Fig. 41 (*lower*).   A detail of the same is shown in Fig. 49.   Appliqué in more net, or in nylon, organdie, etc., would give weight and definition to the design without taking away the transparency. All the above could be worked so as to look satisfactory on both sides.   Beginnings and endings of threads would have to be darned in and suitable stitches chosen so that the em-broidery had no right or wrong side.   A similar technique could be used for a curtain to hang across a window to help obliterate an unpleasant view.

WINDOW CURTAINS

Curtains similarly fall into two main categories, namely opaque and transparent.   The opaque can vary between a heavy furnishing fabric for a living room to a light cotton or gingham for a kitchen.   Design on heavy curtains should be simple and restrained.   An uncluttered design in simple applied shapes, braids and cords would be suitable and would

22. PEACOCK. From curtains designed by Constance Howard for the Piccadilly Hotel, Manchester. The detail shown is on the pelmet of the large set of curtains which hang in the ballroom, known as the "Peacock Room." The design is bold and theatrical, in keeping with its function

look well when the curtains were drawn back during the day. A too fussy design gets lost when the curtains are drawn back and hanging in folds.

Kitchen curtains could have patchwork, appliqué or embroidery designed directly on to gingham checks. They could be made to match tie-on cushions on stools or dining chairs and a covered pelmet could be included in the scheme.

On net curtains, permanently in place across a window, designs of a more pictorial type would be quite suitable, alternatively a repeating geometric pattern could be worked on the counted warp and weft of the net.

CHAIR SEATS AND STOOL TOPS

When embroidery is incorporated into the actual upholstery, as in chair seats and stool tops, it is essential that the embroidery be very hardwearing. For this reason canvas work is the most obvious choice. However, there is no reason why, as is so often the case, the work should be carried out in tent stitch or cross stitch. There is a wide variety of canvas stitches and a mixture of these or one unusual one can be used depending on the type of design being carried out. The stool top in Plate 23 was carried out in encroaching Gobelin stitch giving a thick tapestry-like appearance. Other forms of embroidery could be used (crewel work for instance), but unless the materials used were tough and the stitches firm, the embroidery would not be durable enough to make upholstering worthwhile.

RUGS

The same variety of canvas stitches which are used for upholstery can be worked on a large scale for floor rugs, stair carpets, etc. A soft Persian rug wool is the easiest to sew with and the canvas the one normally used for hook rugs, i.e. three holes to the inch. A contrasting texture may be added with surrey stitch which is worked over a gauge forming a raised pile.

LAMPSHADES

Care should be taken with lampshades to avoid fancy shapes and over-fussy trimmings, otherwise the result will generally be tasteless and vulgar. Especially where the shade is to be embroidered it is far better to stick to plain basic shapes. Designing for a lampshade sets a double problem—the embroidery must look satisfactory during the day and work equally well at night when the light in the lamp is switched on. This is not always easy to accomplish and it is useful to hold the embroidery up against the window or against a strong light occasionally while the work is in progress. If transparent fabrics are used there must be no threads connecting one motif with another, as these will show up when the light is on; also knots should be avoided for starting and finishing threads and all ends trimmed closely. Machine embroidery would be very suitable as it would automatically overcome many of these hazards. If the shade has parallel sides, that is to say if the top circumference is the same as the bottom, then the fabric can be cut in one strip with a single seam. If, on the other hand, the shade is conical in shape, each panel will have to be cut separately and the joins covered with braid or stitches. On a transparent shade the struts inside can be hidden with a lining of ruched net, which will let through the light, at the same time covering the back of the embroidery and the struts of the frame. For big shades, suitable for standard lamps, etc., thick fabrics such as tweed may effectively be used. In these circumstances, however, no light will shine through the fabric and the embroidery need only be considered as it is seen from the outside. Fabrics with unusual textures, raffia cloth, for instance, can be decorated with simple embroidery such as bands of drawn thread, machine stitching, and so on.

If the frame is painted with a rust-proof paint before binding it there is no reason why a lampshade should not be perfectly washable, a point worth bearing in mind when selecting fabrics.

The design of the embroidery can be divided into sections to correspond with the struts of the frame or it can be treated as a plain cylinder ignoring the sections. Although the drawing will probably be done on flat paper it should not be forgotten that the design will never be seen like that on the shade, and that only a part will be seen at a time once the shade is up. The design, while still on paper, should be curved round occasionally into the shape of the lampshade, in order that the true effect may be realized. Many kinds of embroidery are suitable, and much will depend on the scale of the shade and the kind of background fabric being used. On fine materials embroidery incorporating open spaces can be particularly effective with the light shining through the spaces.

23. *Upper:* SOLFLEUR. Garden cushion cover. Designed by Eirian Short for Wm. Briggs & Co. Ltd.
Lower: STOOL TOP IN CANVAS WORK. The entire design is worked in encroaching Gobelin stitch

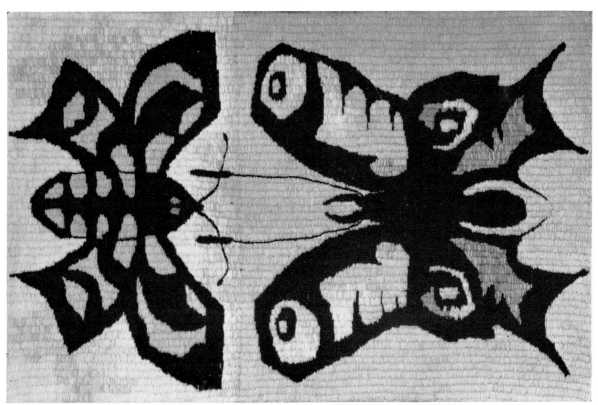

OTHER HOUSEHOLD ARTICLES

English quilting, already dealt with in relation to the bed, has many other uses in the home. Whenever padding is needed for warmth, insulation, weight or comfort, English quilting enables these functions to be carried out in a practical and, at the same time, decorative way. Objects which fall into the above categories include teapot and coffee-pot covers (warmth), hot-water-bottle covers (insulation), quilted hems on curtains (weight), and runners for unupholstered benches and window seats (comfort).

Although traditionally carried out by hand in running or back stitch, the quilting can be done on the sewing machine. Provided the design is simple, using straight or gently curving lines, the machine can be used with the foot on, as for ordinary sewing. Many machines provide a special half-foot and gauge which help to facilitate the work. An experienced machine embroiderer can, by dropping the feed and removing the foot, work the most intricate designs in free running. It must be stressed however that, owing to the thickness of the materials used, this does require real skill and should be left to those who have had a good deal of practice in free embroidery.

Chapter Four

Embroidery as a Medium of Expression

So far this book has dealt with embroidery as an applied decoration, the only criterion being whether the design filled a specific shape satisfactorily; whether mass and line were balanced; colour and tone considered and practical specifications fulfilled. This section of the book deals with work which goes beyond these purely formal qualities, work in which embroidery and fabric collage are used as a means of artistic expression, in other words as "fine art." Because the *main* intent of this type of work is not decoration it does not mean the work cannot incidentally be decorative. Rather, this quality is just one aspect of it. More important is that it is an expression of an idea by the artist; that it has some content. The mistake should not be made of thinking that content in a work of art necessarily means recognizable subject matter. Subject matter, or even complete lack of it, is immaterial; it is the artist's treatment of his *idea* that is important, his vision and the way he translates this vision into some plastic form (painting, sculpture, collage, etc.). In the right hands an apparently trivial subject can be treated profoundly (Van Gogh's painting of his bedroom chair); in the wrong hands a crucifixion can be rendered banal. In the past there have at different times been many conventions as to what constituted suitable subject matter. Whereas in the early days of the Renaissance, landscape was used merely as a background for figure compositions, in the hands of Claude Lorrain in France in the sixteenth century it came into its own right as the sole subject matter for painting of great atmosphere and sensitivity. Still life too, once only an incidental in an interior scene, could under the treatment of a master like Chardin make a beautiful and satisfying picture.

In our time we have come to see that not only can *any subject* properly treated be profound, but that even a picture or sculpture with *no subject* can awaken an emotional response in the onlooker.

As the making of a work of art is the translation into some medium of an artist's ideas there is no reason why this should not be done in fabric and thread as well as it is done in stone or paint. With an increasing interest in the actual surface of the canvas and the introduction of collage into painting, the work of the painter and the embroiderer are very close, and there is no reason why panels in fabric collage and embroidery should not be accepted and considered on precisely the same terms as the best paintings of the day. This statement should not be taken to mean that embroideries should *imitate* paintings, this is not so, fabric must be treated in a way *suitable to its own intrinsic properties* but with a broad vision, sensitivity and imagination.

In order to understand what is being done today it is helpful to examine the past and the reasons why men have produced certain types of work at different times and in different parts of the world. Cavemen, it is thought, painted animals not as decoration for the walls of their caves, but as a form of magic, to gain power over the animals. The ancient Egyptians, on the other hand, depicted their kings in stone and paint to ensure the king's immortality. The work of the cavemen was acutely observed from nature, and captured the muscular strength and grace of the animals; the Egyptian work, on the other hand, was more formal, static, based on knowledge of the human form rather than direct observation. The Chinese, influenced by Buddhism, painted objects for contemplation. They had no wish to depict the outward visual appearance of things but would study a waterfall, mountain, or group of pine trees until they had absorbed its essential character then, with a few deft strokes of the pen or brush, put down a symbol which expressed the essence of the subject. Paradoxically, the symbolic rendering of a mountain by a Chinese or Japanese master can give a feeling of "mountainness" far greater than a naturistically painted study with every blade of grass and piece of rock painted in. All the essentials are stripped away in Oriental Art and the inner nature of the subject is communicated to the onlooker.

Religion has been the driving influence behind many styles

Fig. 50.   Juniper Tree, part of a Chinese scroll.   A highly decorative but at the same time expressive design

of work. The Islamic religion, for instance, forbade the depiction of images and so forced the art of Persia, North Africa and Spain into rich abstract decoration. The Christian religion, on the other hand, fostered the use of the image, Christ Himself being depicted as the centrepiece of most religious paintings. Christian art produced many styles, for example the flat decorative mosaics of the Byzantines, the expressive, human frescoes of Giotto, the lyrical romanticism of Botticelli, the dramatic chiaroscuro of Rembrandt. Another driving force in the West was the struggle to achieve as great a representational realism as possible. This was marked at different periods by the discovery of perspective, the use of modelling to give an appearance of roundness, the use of light and shade, etc., culminating in the scientific breaking up of colour by the impressionists. Towards the end of the nineteenth century as a reaction to four centuries of development along these lines, the striving after external realism was abandoned, and Western art entered a phase of experiment along fresh lines, which is still going on. In a comparatively short time Fauvism, Cubism, Expressionism, Dadaism, Futurism, and Surrealism threw new light on the treatment of subject matter. It was, however, with the abandoning of subject matter altogether and the introduction of pure abstraction that the greatest revolution in art took place. Artists had always of necessity used a certain amount of abstraction simplifying and sometimes distorting the appearance of objects, but it was in 1912 that the first pure abstract was produced, i.e. a picture which had no subject matter at all and which used the components of pictorial composition in the way that a composer of music uses notes, not to represent something external, but as a composition. The painter Mondrian, who was one of the earliest exponents of Abstract art, said of his own work "these works are constructed with lines, surfaces, shapes and colours. They seek to reach beyond human values and attain the infinite and eternal."

Owing to the perishable nature of fabric and threads, far less actual embroidery has come down to us than is known from various evidence to have existed. Historians have to rely greatly for evidence of early work on depictions of embroidery in paintings and carvings, and later on written inventories and historical accounts. It is known, for instance, that the walls of wealthy Anglo-Saxons were covered with sumptuous wall hangings, yet not one piece of domestic embroidery from this period has survived. The few examples of early embroidered hangings and panels which have come down to us have been found preserved in shrines or tombs and many of these are only fragmentary. The walls of the tombs of Scythian warriors were draped with rich hangings with gold plaques attached to them but most of the fabric has rotted away in the specimens which have come to light. One of the hangings of which there is a substantial fragment is a Greco-Scythian one of roughly the time of the birth of Christ. It shows horses and riders, drawn in a flat way, but with overlapping to suggest space. The costumes of the men are covered in allover stylized patterns and there is a border of palmettes and lotus buds. The stitches used are mainly satin stitch and chain stitch, two stitches still in common use today.

After the establishment of the Buddhist religion in China and Japan, many very large embroidered representations of the Buddha were produced. Some are reputed to have been as much as fifty feet high. The ones in existence depict the Buddha life size, the large areas of colour being filled in

Fig. 51.   Detail of the Bayeux Tapestry

solidly in chain, satin, and long-and-short stitch, using a silk thread.   The features of the Buddha and his attendants were worked in split stitch, anticipating the technique of Opus Anglicanum by several hundred years.

The American Indians, the Copts (the early Christians in Egypt), and the people of the Scandinavian countries, used a type of work known as loom embroidery because it was worked while the background fabric was still on the loom on which it had been woven.   The embroidery was worked over the counted thread of the material and could easily be mistaken for tapestry weaving, but it is in fact embroidery (if the stitches were taken away the ground fabric would still be intact).   There is a fine Swedish hanging worked in this method in wool on linen which was discovered in the church of Skog in Helsingland.   The subject is the struggle between paganism and Christianity.   The drawing of the figures is naïve to the point of their being almost geometric but the hanging is both decorative and expressive.

At about the same time (eleventh to twelfth centuries) in England, or possibly France, the so-called Bayeux tapestry was made. It is not a tapestry at all but a piece of pure embroidery and one of the finest examples of the art in existence. It is a pictorial record of the Norman conquest of England and tells the story in the manner of a strip cartoon along the length of 230 feet of linen. It is a wonderful example of flat pattern, figures and objects being simply drawn, the spaces between them carefully considered, each small part of the design relating to the whole. Lettering is incorporated successfully into the design and, in addition to its formal qualities, it tells the story in a lively, expressive and economic way. In England in the thirteenth and fourteenth centuries embroidery rose to be a major art. Indeed it is probably the only time when the fame of a country's embroidery has surpassed that of any other art. Some of the qualities of Opus Anglicanum were discussed in the first chapter. It was certainly a Golden Age in the history of embroidery, when craftsmanship, truth to material, richness of decoration and, above all, content and meaning were fused successfully. Embroidery of a pictorial nature has certainly never again reached the same standard in England.

Embroidered pictures were very popular during the seventeenth century. They fell mainly into two groups: portraits, and scenes with figures. The portraits differed greatly in style. Some, although clever in technique, were nothing more than imitations of paintings, the contours of the face being moulded in light and shade in solid stitchery. Some were in canvas work which necessarily took on a certain stylization because of the method of working. Others were flat and decorative in treatment, somewhat naïve, but with a simple charm and far more feeling for pattern than the imitation oils. Yet another type used was a mixture of techniques, working the portrait partly in outline, partly in solid stitchery and adding decorative touches of padding, loops of bound wire or parchment, braids and gimps. These were the forerunners of stump work which was an embroidery peculiar to England of the seventeenth century which carried these techniques to grotesque extremes. Most stump work pictures, whether they be portraits, biblical or mythological scenes, are excessively padded, lacking in any sense of scale or design and generally tasteless, but because of their unsimilarity to embroidery before or since have a certain period charm. Biblical and mythological subjects were popular also for canvas work pictures of a more two dimensional nature. These pictures were on a small scale, but this century also saw the working of big wall hangings in the style afterwards known as "Jacobean." These, inspired by the Oriental Tree of Life, were of exotic plant shapes and were worked in crewel wool on twill. The hangings, worked in strong colours, were lively and vigorous, but the many weak imitations of this style over the years have debased the name of Jacobean embroidery. Embroidered pictures were again in vogue at the end of the eighteenth century. One type consisted of groups of figures worked in silk on a white satin background with the hands and faces painted in in watercolour. Copies of contemporary engravings, in black silk, were also popular, but these, of course, had no artistic merit. This is also the time when Mary Linwood rose to fame with her exact copies of famous contemporary paintings. Clever though these "paintings with the needle" are, they surely stand as one of the prime examples of what *not* to do in embroidery.

The early Victorian period saw the birth of Berlin wool work, which soon spread to become an absolute craze, to the exclusion of almost every other kind of embroidery. That meant that very little original design was used in the making of pictures. Most people were content to copy from charts the hackneyed and unsuitable Berlin designs. However, about 1856 William Morris started taking an interest in embroidery, and he and his wife made some experimental pieces, dying their own worsted wools and unpicking old embroideries to learn about the techniques. By 1860 he was ready to design and execute a set of hangings for the Red House built for him by Philip Webb. Some of these had floral subjects, the rest consisted of a set of figures based on Chaucer's *Illustrious Women*. Each figure was worked on linen in crewel wools with some silk and metal threads, then cut out and applied to a blue woollen background which had already been embroidered with a simple design of coiling stems and flowers. When, in 1861, Morris and his partners set up workshops, they undertook to execute any kind of embroidery, and employed skilled needlewomen to do so, although members of the family and friends helped in the carrying out of the designs. As some of the hangings were nine or ten feet long, covered with intricate designs and embroidered entirely by hand, they must have entailed a terrific amount of work. As the firm also sold ready traced materials and supplied the threads for working them, Morris's influence was widespread.

It was mainly due to Morris's influence that the Royal School of Needlework was formed in 1872. He was also on

24. WHITE SUN by Eirian Short. The panel makes use of a technique closely allied to paper sculpture. The fabric, previously backed with an iron-on interlining, is cut with a razor blade and pressed. Chain stitch is worked on the Cornely machine and pearls and long bugle beads are added

the committee of the Arts and Crafts Exhibition Society, formed in 1888, which still holds exhibitions every two or three years, and has always included embroideries. In the early days of the Society, many of the leading designers of the day exhibited embroideries—Morris himself, Burne Jones, Lewis F. Day and Walter Crane.

In the 1890s the Art Nouveau Movement came into being in the British Isles and Western Europe, differing in detail from country to country but bearing general characteristics.

25. *Upper:* WAVE BREAKING, by Eirian Short. The panel, now in the possession of Leicestershire Education Committee, is worked in a combination of appliqué, hand and machine embroidery. *Lower:* ST. IVES. An impression of houses by the sea, by Ioné Dorrington

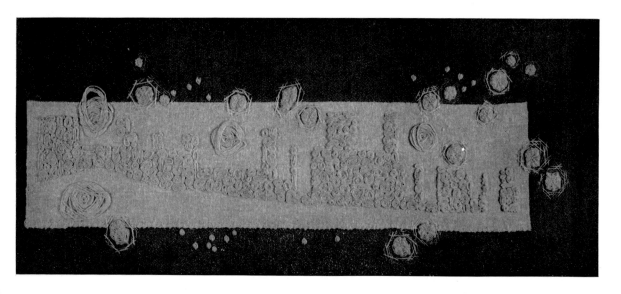

26. *Upper:* SURGE. Fabric collage by Margaret Kaye. *Lower:* WROUGHT IRON GATE, by Eirian Short. Appliqué and chain stitch on the Cornely machine. (*In the possession of Copthall County Grammar School*)

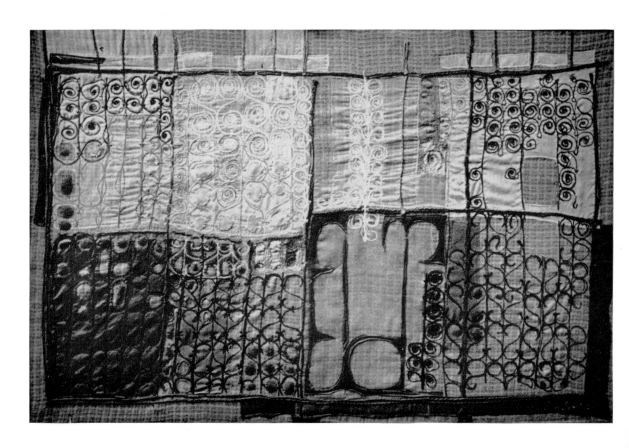

Most of the architects and designers in this movement designed for embroidery. One particular branch of the movement was to have a particular effect upon embroidery design, that of the Glasgow school, under Charles Rennie Mackintosh. Two women played a leading part in the movement, Jessie Newberry, wife of the principal of Glasgow Art School, and Ann Macbeth. They stressed certain principles which could not fail to have a good effect on embroidery design and, although they first exhibited the new style before the death of Victoria, its influence was still strong in the 1920s. They stressed that embroidery should not imitate painting, that the design should spring from the technique itself. In figure work they depicted form with line rather than shading, and avoided naturalistic flesh tints. The stylized plant forms of the Art Nouveau style were used, but in the Glasgow school the style was leavened with an architectural simplicity, a

27. THIEVING MAGPIE. Collage by Selina Rand, aged ten years, a pupil at Brooklands Park Primary School, Blackheath

28. SWAN AND COCKEREL, by
Margaret Kaye

Bɪʀᴅ, by Margaret Kaye

feeling for the horizontal and perpendicular. It was also emphasized that embroidered panels and hangings must be designed in relation to architecture and interior decoration, and it is one of the characteristics of the work of this period that buildings, furniture, embroidery, ornaments, and jewellery all harmonized.

The invention of sewing and embroidery machines during the Victorian era had its effect mainly on dress and furnishings. There was a brief spell before the First World War when machine-embroidered pictures were produced on the ordinary sewing machine and sold, but it was not until the late 'twenties and early 'thirties that the possibilities of the machine as a really creative medium were realized. In 1936 the Art Schools gave it official recognition and it was included in the Ministry's examinations. Today it is recognized that machine embroidery is just another facet of embroidery as a whole, not a thing to be separately classified, and that the

29. BLACK BEAUTY, by Eirian Short. The beads are from a collection made over many years and include jet, wood and black glass. P.V.C. in a stamped crocodile pattern (cut from an old raincoat) is also used

30. *Upper:* Sun 3, by Rosalind Floyd.   The panel, one of a series on the subject, makes interesting use of different levels and cut-away fabric; *Lower:* Pile Up, by Anne Butler.   Another experimental technique, using nails and crumpled fabric.   The method of working was as follows: Appliqué in contrasting fabrics and pieces of leather was completed; the panel was then mounted on to a wooden board and nails hammered into the surface, leaving part of each nail projecting.   Threads were wound from one nail to another on the surface.   The heads of the nails were painted to fit in to the colour scheme

machine itself is a tool which can be used as creatively as a needle in the hand of an artist. Work done at the present time is far less conscious of technique and uses hand embroidery, machine embroidery, collage and experimental methods as a means rather than an end in themselves. This reflects the trends in modern painting and sculpture which make use of natural and manufactured objects, combinations of different media, such as collage and painting, sculpture and painting, etc. Since the Second World War there has been a definite Renaissance in the art of embroidery. In the field of interior decoration and furnishing the influence was mainly Swedish, and like Swedish designs in other fields, was simple, tasteful but rather dull. A far more vigorous work has sprung up indigenously, two pioneers of the movement being Margaret Kaye and Constance Howard. With their own vastly different styles these two have, by direct teaching in the Art schools, and by showing their work in galleries, influenced a whole new school of lively designers in the media of embroidery and collage.

Before beginning a picture, panel, or hanging the designer should have a clear idea in his mind of what exactly is involved. The aim is not to reproduce some subject realistically on fabric. Even when a recognizable subject is used the objective is not to make a life-like representation of it. For one thing, the invention of the camera has made faithful copying for the sake of recording pointless. For another, as discussed in Chapter I, it is not in keeping with the aims and the intrinsic character of embroidery to strive for realistic three-dimensional effects. A picture has an existence of its own and stands or falls by how successful it is *as a picture*, not on the subject that it represents. The subject may have to be drastically simplified, or even distorted to make the picture "work." Someone walking into Matisse's studio remarked, pointing to a picture on an easel, "Surely the arm of this woman is much too long." To which Matisse replied, "Madame, you are mistaken, this is not a woman, this is a picture." It is not enough to make a mere decoration. To qualify as a work of art there must be some content beyond that of the formal qualities of line, mass, colour and texture. According to Arnheim, "Every work of art must express something. The content of the work must go beyond the presentation of the objects of which the work consists. This must produce an experience in the onlooker if it is to be an artistic expression."

A picture then is the fusion of two qualities: the formal and the expressive, both of which are important. A picture which has a good formal arrangement but expresses nothing becomes just a pattern. A picture which is expressive but without the control of visual elements has no impact. In the past, too many embroidered pictures have fitted into the first category, being decorative illustrations. This is now being rectified by the best of our designers who have abandoned the rather "twee" decorative type of embroidered picture for work of a more serious nature. The concept of the idea must be a *pictorial* and not a *literary* one. To understand the difference, compare the way two painters have depicted grief (Plate 31). In Picasso's "Weeping Woman" the essence of grief is expressed in the distorted face, the way the features are arranged, in the angular shapes that emphasize the emotion. This puts over the idea of grief far more strongly than a straightforward rendering of a woman in tears. The artist has by the forms and composition he has used, heightened the emotional content of the picture. This is an instance of an idea conceived pictorially. Compare this with Landseer's "The Old Shepherd's Chief Mourner" which portrays a sheepdog, head resting on his dead master's bed. Here there is nothing in the composition to suggest grief, nothing of tension in the forms. To get its message over, the picture relies on the sentimental association in our minds of a dog mourning its master. The idea is implanted purely by literary association, and not by what the eye sees in the painting. It is the function of the artist to convey *visually* what the writer conveys in *words*.

The choice of subject (or absence of subject) is immaterial. It is the treatment that is important. Ben Shahn has said "Whatever crosses the human mind is fit content for art." Subject matter can be treated in one of two ways, by image, i.e. by depicting the subject directly, or by symbol, i.e. using some format to represent the idea of the subject. Direct image does not imply slavish copying from the subject, there is bound to be selection and possibly distortion in all perceptive representation. Symbolism is used largely in religious work. In Christianity alone the symbols are

31. *Upper:* THE WEEPING WOMAN,
by Picasso. (*By courtesy of the
Penrose Collection* and S.P.A.D.E.M.
of Paris); *Lower:* THE OLD SHEP-
HERD'S CHIEF MOURNER, by Sir Edwin
Landseer. (*By courtesy of the Victoria
and Albert Museum*). Both pictures
depict grief, but in one (Picasso) the
emotion is conveyed by the tortured
character of the composition, in the
other (Landseer) by sentimental
literary association

countless, such as the phoenix—symbolizing reincarnation, the peacock—immortality, the ship—Christianity weathering the storm, and so on. Symbolism is also found in primitive work, a circle representing the sun, a wavy line a snake, etc. A symbol, by its very economy, often has more impact than a direct image. A crown of thorns, in itself a simple motif, can conjure up the suffering on the Cross more vividly than many an elaborate crucifixion scene.

Between figurative art and pure abstraction there are a number of stages. The subject may be slightly simplified or distorted in the interest of design or it can be abstracted to such an extent that it is no longer recognizable (*see* "Treatment of the Human Figure," Fig. 52), but in either case the process is one of the translation of subject matter into pictorial form. With a pure abstract there is no subject matter, the design springs entirely from the mind of the artist. The starting-off point, however, is incidental, so too is the technique employed. The final result is the only thing that matters. The knowledge of the various techniques at the embroiderer's command should be used as a means to an end and never as an end in themselves. The criterion should be whether this particular stitch or that particular method gives the required effect in any particular instance. In other words, technical knowledge should be a tool in the hand of the artist rather than a controlling influence.

Although it is stressed that there is no such thing as a hard and fast rule, there are guiding principles which it is well to keep in mind when planning a picture, panel or hanging. The use of the ground fabric as a window should be avoided (i.e. giving an illusion of looking at a scene in depth). A certain amount of depth can be suggested by overlapping or by variations in size without violating the two-dimensional nature of the ground (*see* Figs. 15, *centre* and *right*). Modelling, i.e. shading to give a feeling of roundness, is also out of character with the two-dimensional nature of embroidery. When depicting three-dimensional objects a scheme must be found to suggest the character of the object without giving the illusion that "it could be picked off the background."

Although contrasts in texture add interest to a panel, careful thought should be given to the use of textural materials used in a realistic way. In primitive and peasant

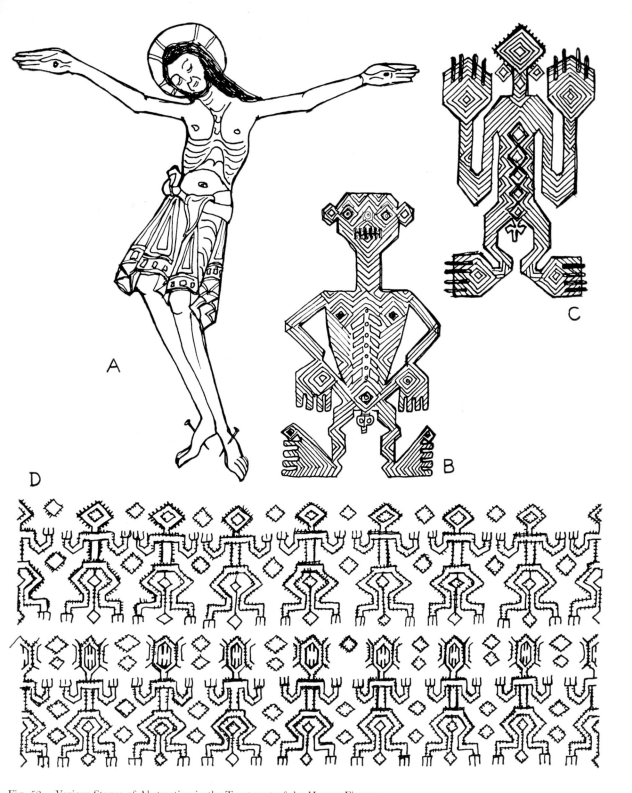

Fig. 52.   Various Stages of Abstraction in the Treatment of the Human Figure:
(A) Decorative but fairly naturalistic Christ-figure from mediaeval manuscript.   (B) Flat treatment, using anatomical features as pattern.   (C) Human figure further abstracted; ears, eyes, nose etc. have disappeared and head is symbolized by a geometric shape. (D) Repeat pattern using the figure in so abstracted a form that it reads purely as a design motif.   (B), (C) and (D) are taken from Indonesian Textiles

work realistic materials such as feathers for birds and fur for animals are sometimes used with good effect, adding to the naiveté and charm of the work. Their introdution into a more sohpisticated style of work, however, can look tawdry. It is generally better to use such items as feathers and furs purely for their textural qualities, rather than for their natural connotations. Realistic *relief* should also be treated with caution. Good examples can be found, such as the exquisitely delicate faces in Chinese embroideries or the vital, exuberant stump work on Hungarian ecclesiastical work; but it *can* destroy the quality of illusion inherent in a work of art. The beginner is advised to use padding, relief and different levels to add variety and interest rather than to simulate reality.

Technique

However much the importance of concept in a work of art is stressed, it is essential to have a certain amount of technical knowledge in order to be able to translate that concept into tangible form. A sound knowledge of the medium and its characteristics ensures that (a) the effect aimed at is achieved, (b) that this is brought about in the easiest way, and (c) that the work when completed will be durable. The basic procedures in putting together a fabric picture, panel or hanging are discussed below.

1. *The Design*. The method of arriving at the design is a matter of individual choice. Some designers work out the design in detail, either in colour or monochrome, using paints, coloured paper, inks, etc. Others prefer to work directly in fabric, often letting the fabrics, threads, and other materials suggest much of the design. A lot depends on personal preference and the method used may also depend to some extent on the type of design. A precise "hard edge" design could well be worked out on paper and traced accurately on to fabric; a free, spontaneous composition, depending perhaps on exciting contrast of texture, would obviously grow naturally out of the materials as they were handled. Both methods have advantages and disadvantages. In the first, care must be taken to avoid niggly detail and a temptation to imitate a pencil line or brush stroke exactly, rather than to translate it into terms of embroidery or collage. Also an

open mind must be kept throughout. It must not be thought that because the design is carefully worked out on paper that there will be no alteration needed when working in fabric and thread. The characteristics intrinsic in fabric and thread will obviously impose themselves on the design, and alterations will have to be made accordingly. The chief disadvantage of the second, direct, method as far as the inexperienced designer is concerned, is that there is bound to be a certain wastage of material in trial and error. This, however, becomes less with experience and is, anyway, compensated for in the extra spontaneity and freedom of the finished work.

2. *Cutting Out.* The background fabric should always be cut larger than the required picture area. Whether the finished work is to be mounted on hardboard, stretched on a frame or backed, as a hanging, some extra material will be needed for turning in. Also there is a tendency for a design to spread in the working out, and to have too small a background cramps the style and often makes alterations in the design impossible. In an emergency, extra pieces can be attached round the edges, but this is not as satisfactory as allowing plenty of material in the first place. In order that applied pieces should lie flat when sewn down, they should be cut with the grain running vertically and horizontally to match the warp and weft of the ground fabric. Pieces laid on the cross pucker and are difficult to sew down. On small pieces of fabric this is not so important and there are times, of course, when a puckered effect is deliberately aimed at. Certain unwoven materials, such as felt, have no grain and will lie equally well in any position. It is not necessary to have turnings in pictorial work, and so all pieces can be cut exactly to size.

3. *Attaching Materials to the Background.* It is advisable to pin the whole composition in place before any sewing down is done. When the pieces are firmly pinned in position the work should be hung on the wall and looked at from a distance, when any faults in the design should become apparent. Alteration can easily be made at this stage. Except in the special circumstances enumerated below, sticking or gluing materials is not advised. It is messy, often irrevocable, and, worst of all, makes the materials flat and

lifeless. A colourless rubber solution can, however, be used in some instances. When fabrics of a fraying nature have to be cut out with precise detail a thin layer of rubber solution spread on the back of the fabric and allowed to dry before cutting will eliminate fraying. It is also useful for holding small pieces on temporarily. Scraps of kid or leather, sequins, or buttons can be held in place with a spot of rubber solution until they can be more firmly attached by sewing.

Normally the most satisfactory method is to tack all pieces in position, and then sew them down by hand or machine. Again each method has advantages and disadvantages. Machining is much quicker and is thoroughly recommended for large panels which are viewed from a distance. On small pictures of a delicate nature, however, machine stitching can give too hard an outline, and herringboning, hemming, or running stitch in a fine thread may be more unobtrusive. Where a swing needle machine is available, a zig-zag stitch can be used for fraying fabrics, but for felt or leather, a straight stitch just inside the edge is satisfactory.

4. *Embroidery*. If hand and machine embroidery are being used it will be found more convenient to work any machine embroidery before that done by hand. For machine embroidery it is often necessary to use a tambour frame and this is awkward where there are already chunky stitches on the fabric. Once any machine embroidery is done the work can, if needed, be fixed up in a slate (rectangular) frame for the addition of any hand embroidery or beading. Beads, if used, should always be put on last as the sewing thread catches on them during the working.

A certain amount of puckering is almost inevitable where a mixture of techniques is used. Putting the work into a frame at the beginning is impractical if any machine embroidery is contemplated, so the only solution is to use as a background a sound fabric which can be damped and stretched once the work is completed. Tweed, hessian, woollen dress fabrics, furnishing fabrics, are all suitable. To be avoided are taffettas, organdies and such materials that split easily when stretched. Once the work is complete it should be stretched face upwards over damp blotting paper with drawing pins fixed close together around the edges. Small pieces can be stretched on a drawing board; for large hangings the

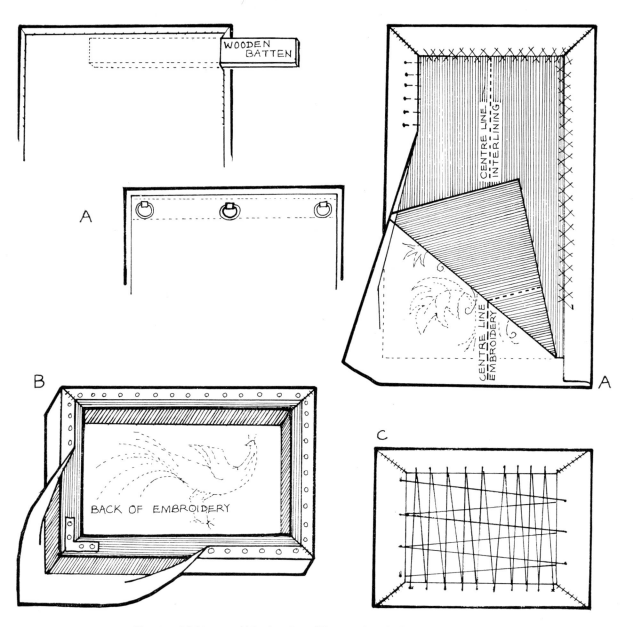

Fig. 53. Making up: (A) a hanging; (B) a panel; and (C) a small picture

floor may have to be used. As soon as the work is dry it can be removed and made up into a panel or hanging.

5. *Making up* (Fig. 53). Large panels are best tacked on to a wooden stretcher or frame. This can easily be made with strips of battening supported at the corners by metal brackets. A panel of this kind can easily be framed with a strip of brass or aluminium edging or with a batten of natural wood.

Small pictures suitable for framing under glass can simply be laced over a piece of hardboard cut to fit the frame. Making up a hanging is a more complicated affair and needs to be done carefully if the work is to hang well. Many well-designed hangings are ruined by being carelessly made up. An accurate centre line should be tacked down the centre of the hanging and of the interlining, which could be of heavy vilene or canvas. The interlining should be the exact proposed size of the finished work. The embroidery should be laid out face downward and the interlining placed on top, centre tackings matching. The edge of the hanging is then turned over on to the interlining and caught down taking care to sew only through the interlining. The backing is then slip-stitched into position, being turned in to within about a quarter of an inch of the edge of the hanging. A space may be left at the top to slip in a batten of wood, into which may be screwed rings for hanging the finished work. Fancy headings of tabs and rings are not recommended, they look fussy and old-fashioned. The hanging will look far better as a simple rectangle, with no unnecessary details to distract the eye from the design.

Ecclesiastical Embroidery

Religion has inspired some of the greatest works of art in the past in painting, sculpture, architecture, and embroidery. In widely differing civilizations, with their various religions, embroidery has been closely connected with religious ritual. When cloth itself was plain, it was the addition of embroidery, with gold and precious stones, which made it worthy of the high use to which it was put in religious ceremonies. Although most of the great masterpieces were produced for the church itself, it is fascinating to trace the religious symbols used, simply and humbly, in the every-day embroidery of peasants. For instance, the lily pot, one of the symbols of the Virgin Mary, and the pomegranate, the symbol of future life, are often found in peasant work. Moorish or Spanish embroidery will show any animals or birds with their heads severed because the Mohammedan religion forbade the depicting of living creatures. Thus embroidery not directly connected with the church shows the influence of the religion of those who worked it (Fig. 54).

Fig. 54.   Lamb and Flag Motif from Spanish Peasant Shirt

How much greater is the opportunity when working directly for the church to make full use of its rich symbolism, combining decoration with a deeper spiritual meaning. The Christian religion has a vast store of symbols, some of which go back to pagan times.   Some of these, the fish, for instance, were adopted by the Early Christians while they were still worshipping in secret.   Others were incorporated into secular decoration to escape detection.   An example is the cross portrayed as the mast of a ship.   Later, when the Christian religion was accepted and worship became open, Christian symbols were included in decorative work in a great variety of media: ivory carvings, enamels, stained glass, manuscripts, etc.

A symbol is a powerful factor in design, because it can put over a complex meaning in a simple visual form.   Its very economy gives it impact.   It can convey an abstract *idea*— the circle for instance, having no beginning and no end, symbolizes eternal life.   Or it can convey an event and all its associations—the cross or the crown of thorns symbolize the suffering of the crucifixion.   The cock represents Peter's repentance.   Some symbols are attributed personally to different saints. St. Catherine carries a wheel of torture, St. Cecilia a musical instrument. Monograms and initial letters are used too, Alpha and Omega, the first and last letters of the Greek alphabet ($A\Omega$), symbolize the beginning and the end. I H S, P X are both sacred monograms of Christ himself. The four apostles, Matthew, Mark, Luke and John, are depicted respectively as an angel, a winged lion, a winged bull and an eagle. Some emblems will appeal to the embroiderer because of their obvious decorative qualities, for example the fountain, the pomegranate, the tree of life. More abstract symbolism might be felt to be appropriate for modern churches, though there is no reason why a traditional figurative symbol should not be designed in such a way as to be in keeping with the most experimental modern church building. It cannot be stressed too often that it is the treatment which is important, not the subject matter.

When recognizable figurative symbols are used the meaning is usually clear. An equally powerful response can be awakened in the onlooker by an abstract design. In this no symbols with literal meanings are used; the meaning is conveyed by colour and shape and the emotions which they arouse in the viewer. Most colours have symbolic associations. Red, for instance, typifies passion, fire; green—growth, birth; white—purity, innocence; purple—majesty, and so on. Shapes and the direction of line also arouse definite sensations in the onlooker. A tall triangle gives a feeling of thrusting upwards; a circle suggests completeness, perfection; diagonal lines give an impression of urgency, a horizontal line conveys serenity, peace. And so, by abstract arrangements of colour and shape, an emotional response can be aroused in the viewer as strong as any produced by a recognizable figurative image.

Many of the problems encountered in designing for the church are similar to those in other fields of work, but some are peculiar to ecclesiastical work and, therefore, need special consideration. The purpose of the work should be kept in mind. The church is built as a temple in which God is glorified and worshipped, and also as a quiet place for meditation. Any embroidery in the church should contribute to rather than detract from these purposes. Anything cheap, shoddy, shallow or clever to a degree of slickness, is out of place. This does not mean that work should be in any way

Fig. 55. Altar Frontal Designed by George Pace for the Welsh Guards Chapel, Llandaff Cathedral
The embroidery was carried out by the Royal School of Needlework

namby-pamby. Indeed it should be vigorous, powerful and uplifting. Pugin, the great Gothic revival architect of the nineteenth century, wrote in 1844, "Every ornament to deserve the name must possess an appropriate meaning, and be introduced with an intelligent purpose, and on reasonable grounds." This statement still holds good for present-day ecclesiastical design.

Most ecclesiastical embroidery, apart from the altar linen, is made to be seen from a distance, consequently fine stitchery and subtle nuances of design are wasted. The altar is the focal point of the church both by placing and association so that the design needs to be strong. If there is a stained-glass window above the altar, the frontal could link up with it in colour, otherwise the two vie for attention. There is often one dominant colour in the window which could be used as the background for the altar frontal. The shape and size of the altar frontal make it suitable for designs in a variety of arrangements. The frontal may be divided into a number of panels which need not necessarily be equal, or one bold motif or group of motifs may be placed on a plain background. Another solution is to use a repeating motif as in the George Pace frontal at Llandaff (Fig. 55). A well-designed pictorial subject could fill the space well, as also an expressive abstract. Ideas could be based on some architectural feature, such as stone or wood carving, tiles or window tracery which form part of the building. As the altar frontal is a fixture, there is no limit to the kind of materials which can be used, unlike those for the vestments which have to drape and are handled frequently. This leaves the designer free to experiment with unusual-textured fabrics, and a variety of free techniques.

Traditionally, the choice of colour is not quite so free. Since the end of the middle ages the Church has specified that certain colours be used at different seasons and on saints' days. These "liturgical" colours consist of white, gold, red, blue, purple, green, black and yellow. Though this may sound limiting, within these bounds there can be endless variations. Green, for example, could be interpreted as, say olive green, a bright grass green, or a bluey bottle green, and still come within the meaning of liturgical green. Many small churches obviously cannot afford to have different sets of vestments for each season and have to compromise, also there is today a trend away from strict adherence to liturgical colours. Provided the embroidery is fitting for its purpose, it is more important to have vigour and sincerity than it is to stick closely to traditional conventions.

The cope, a semi-circular garment worn draped over the shoulders with the straight edges meeting down the front, also offers scope for many different arrangements of decoration. In the Middle Ages, arcading, allover patterns of quatrefoils, circles and star shapes and the tree of Jesse were popular. Today a simpler scheme is sometimes preferred, perhaps one richly embroidered shape on the centre back and shoulders, tailing off down the arms and back rather than ending suddenly, in which case the hood would be omitted. On the other hand, if the hood is retained, this and the orphrey could be decorated but the body of the cope left plain. In this case a scattered motif or motifs of different sizes, or a design radiating from the neck or growing upwards from the hem would be equally appropriate. The two points to bear in mind are that the cope is seen mostly from the back and that it falls in folds.

The same applies to the gothic-shaped chasuble, the most usual shape in use today. This is an interesting shape to design for and it is suggested that many thumbnail sketches of the shape be made, and different arrangements for the embroidery tried out (Fig. 56). The stole and maniple are usually made to form a set with the chasuble. In recent years the shape of the stole has become simplified to an almost straight strip, with a little shaping for the neck; design can be allover or at the ends only, since these are the only parts which show in use.

Other articles which give great scope to the embroidery designer are kneelers, banners and dossal hangings. Kneelers are usually worked in canvas work and can be designed as a set, each kneeler individual in design but contributing to the general scheme. Banners often incorporate lettering, which is an interesting challenge to the designer—

32. *Upper:* ALTAR FRONTAL. Designed by Constance Howard for the Chapel of Makerere College, Kampala, Uganda. The design is based on an African motif, taken from a book on African painting by Margaret Trowell.
Lower: ECCLESIASTICAL PANEL based on Christian symbolism. Designed and worked by Josephine Canty

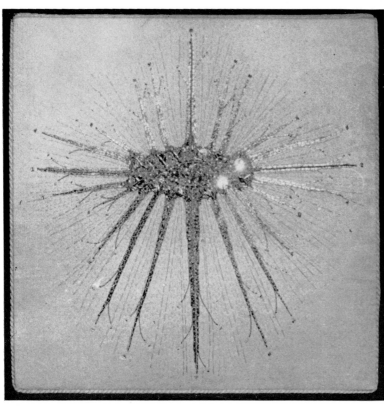

Fig. 56.   Three Chasuble Designs Based on the Cross

to produce something which is at the same time legible and decorative.   Individual letters can indeed be used as units of design and treated in an abstract way with very exciting results.   The dossal can be in the form of a small hanging or panel, or it can be replaced by a hanging covering the entire wall behind the altar, as does the Sutherland tapestry at Coventry Cathedral.   In the latter case the dossal could be the foundation for a design of great scale and power.

The treatment of figure subjects in ecclesiastical embroidery needs careful consideration.   Too often a designer who happily experiments with plant forms and animals will, when confronted with the human figure, resort to the hackneyed, pseudo-medieval figure in the nebulous draped garment which is so often seen in church work.   Surely there must be some way of treating the human figure which is in

34. *Upper:* Detail of Cope opposite;
Lower: Motif on Morse (Fastening Panel)

35. COPE, by Barbara Dawson, gold work on a white background (*By courtesy of the Crafts Council of Great Britain*)

character with contemporary trends. Is there a pointer in the painting and sculpture of the day? Some of the following could be adapted successfully to embroidery—simultaneous views of profile and front view incorporated into one figure, as in many of Picasso's works; evocative, fragmented, barely suggested figures such as Bacon's; monumental, almost abstract figures with spaces playing as important a part as the solid forms as in Henry Moore's sculpture. If painters and sculptors can present the figure in a new and highly personal way, surely it is not beyond the skill and vision of the embroidery and collage designer to do likewise, always keeping in mind the particular character of the medium.

England is rich in city and country churches, but how rarely does the embroidery seen in them live up to the standard of the architecture. Although in the structure of the church there may be many styles spanning hundreds of years, there seems to be a reluctance to work embroidery in the present-day manner. Instead it seems to be thought more suitable to imitate the medieval or even the Victorian idea of the medieval! This is quite illogical. If a fifteenth century window can take its place in a twelfth century church, why should a twentieth century piece of embroidery not do so equally well. Fashion and style are always changing and any work which merely copies the style of a past era is bound to lack conviction. Ideas may be absorbed from historical pieces and these may form the starting point for a design, but unless the work itself bears the stamp of the time in which it was carried out it lacks truth and conviction. In a new church the problems are simplified. The design for the embroideries can be planned from the beginning as an integral part of the whole church. Sometimes the architect designs the embroidery himself, the work being carried out by a professional or by a team of voluntary workers. George Pace's altar frontal in the Guards Chapel at Llandaff Cathedral, carried out by the Royal School of Needlework, is a good example. The design is based on the motif which is used for the iron work and candlesticks, giving a feeling of unity in the small chapel. It is even more satisfactory for the work to be designed by the embroiderer who is to carry it out, but in consultation with the architect. In this way it is possible to have a more spontaneous design as much of it will develop in the actual working. Because work for the church is imbued with spiritual significance, this does not mean that it need be in any way ostentatious. Matisse, as the culmination of a lifetime's painting, designed, at Vence, a church of utter simplicity. The stained glass, the decorations on the walls, the mosaics and the vestments are almost childlike in their simplicity of form and clarity of colour, but this is far from being naïve work. It is, in fact, highly sophisticated, being stripped of all inessentials, and conveying its message with complete sincerity and conviction and

36. TWO SETS OF VESTMENTS.
Gouache designs by Matisse in the Musée Matisse,
Vence.   Each set consists of chasuble, stole, maniple,
burse and veil. (© S.P.A.D.E.M. Paris, 1967.   *By
courtesy of the Musée Matisse*)

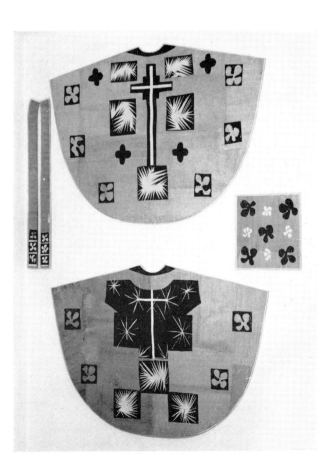

with the greatest economy of means. It is obvious from looking at work like this at Vence, and from studying much Oriental work, that this doing away with inessentials and getting to the essence of an idea is instrumental in producing work of great power. It is not, as might be supposed, a state which is easily attained, but is reached after years of thinking about and experimenting with the problems of conveying an idea in plastic form.

There is a lesson here for the embroiderer. Far too much embroidery is designed in a "bitty" way; too much attention being paid to the actual stitches, areas often being broken up for no better reason than to show a variety of techniques. How much more powerful is the broad vision, the simple, overall conception of how the work will look from a distance.

Useful Reference Books

Hand Embroidery

Anchor Manual of Needlework   J. & P. Coates

CHRISTIE, MRS. ARCHIBALD   *Samplers and Stitches*   Batsford

FRY, GLADYS WINDSOR   *Embroidery and Needlework*   Pitman

HOWARD, CONSTANCE   *Inspiration for Embroidery*   Batsford

THOMAS, MARY   *Dictionary of Embroidery Stitches*   Hodder & Stoughton

THOMAS, MARY   *Embroidery Book*   Hodder & Stoughton

WADE, VICTORIA   *The Basic Stitches of Embroidery*   Victoria and Albert Museum

Ecclesiastical Embroidery

DEAN, BERYL   *Church Needlework*   Batsford

DEAN, BERYL   *Ecclesiastical Embroidery*   Batsford

Machine Embroidery

BENSON, DOROTHY   *Your Machine Embroidery*   Sylvan Press

GRAY, JENNIFER   *Machine Embroidery*   Batsford

RISLEY, CHRISTINE   *Machine Embroidery*   Vista Books

List of Suppliers

Embroidery Threads and Materials
Needlewoman Ltd, 146 Regent Street, London, W.1.
Harrods Ltd, Knightsbridge, London, S.W.1.
Dryad Ltd, 22 Bloomsbury Street, London, W.C.1.

D.M.C. Threads (wholesale) for hand and machine embroidery
M.R. Ltd, 1A Thornford Road, London, S.E.13.

Metal Threads
Toye, Kenning and Spencer Ltd, Regalia House, Red Lion Square, London, W.C.1.
Louis Grosse Ltd, 36 Manchester Street, London, W.1.
Needlewoman Ltd, see above.

Machine Embroidery Cottons
Necchi Sewing Machines Ltd, 76 Oxford Street, London, W.1.

Beads and Trimmings
Ells & Farrier Ltd, 5 Princes Street, London, W.1.
Bourne & Hollingsworth Ltd, Oxford Street, London, W.1.
Needlewoman Ltd, see above.

Plastics
B. & G. (Leathercloth) Ltd, 147 Cleveland Street, London, W.1.

Leathers including gold and silver kid
Light Leathers Ltd, 16 Soho Square, London, W.1.

Interlinings, Vanishing Muslin, etc.
MacCulloch and Wallis Ltd, 25 Dering Street, London W.1.

Fabrics: a wide selection of colours in dress and furnishing fabrics at reasonable prices
John Lewis & Co Ltd, Oxford Street, London, W.1.

Index